# Creative Kindness

Share your hands and heart with those in need…these inspirational stories and over a dozen practical projects will show you how.

By Nancy Zieman with Gail Brown

Published by

 **krause publications**
An F&W Publications Company

700 East State Street • Iola, WI 54990-0001
715-445-2214 • 888-457-2873
www.krause.com

Please call or write for our free catalog of publications. Our toll-free number to place an order or obtain a free catalog is 800-258-0929, or please use our regular business telephone 715-445-2214.

ISBN: 0-87349-696-5

Printed in the United States of America

# Contents

# Creative Kindness:
## People and Projects Making a Difference—
## And How You Can, Too

ANOTHER REQUEST for a donation was placed on my desk. In the letter, Jackie Bushong-Martin described how her volunteers made and shipped hundreds of school uniforms to poor Haitian children (see page 56).

How could I—or just about anyone, for that matter—not be touched by her words, or the photos of these children smiling proudly in their new uniforms? Their young, hopeful faces and the accompanying request for a donation were impossible to file away and forget.

Almost from the moment I first stepped before the TV camera, I began to receive similarly inspiring letters from charities, asking for fabric, sewing supplies and money. My staff and I attempted to handle the literally thousands of requests from deserving causes that have poured in for the last 20 years.

But as our database of charities grew, so did my frustration. How could I and our company best assist and endow these generous efforts? How could I say "no" to these ordinary people doing such extraordinary deeds for others?

*Nancy Zieman, host of public TV show, Sewing with Nancy, and the owner of Nancy's Notions.*

### Sharing a 'Smile'
I often felt like the Dutch boy with his finger in the dike. Materials and money contributions could provide welcome but only short-term assistance.

Then one day the answer dawned on me: *Pass along these stories of creative kindness so that others would be inspired to contribute—and they, in turn, would inspire even more people.*

Because my *Sewing with Nancy* TV show and Nancy's Notions® mail-order business cater to those who sew, quilt and craft, I could focus my efforts on matching people with those particular skills with those in need of them.

Every day, through the mail, TV and the Internet, I connected with millions in the U.S., Canada and around the world. I was convinced that

once my viewers and customers heard that there are people who need their time and talents, they would respond.

I was also convinced, more than ever, that each of us needs to feel we are touching another person's life. I knew there was an untapped willingness to put our hands, our hearts and the creativity that lives in all of us to work making a better world.

Now that I knew what I had to do, it was time for action. Our first public rollout was the "Sew a Smile" three-part series for my *Sewing with Nancy* program. In this series, I reported on nine worthy causes, many of which are recapped and updated in this book.

### Unprecedented Response
But reporting was only the first step. The second was to provide action plans for viewers—ways to connect with charities in need of people with sewing, crocheting, knitting and organizational skills, plus tips for making similar versions of the featured projects.

My newly energized staff and I dedicated ourselves to making "Sew a Smile" a shot of adrenaline for viewers. In February 1998, the series was uplinked to public television stations nationwide.

*"Then one day the answer dawned on me: Pass along these stories of creative kindness so that others would be inspired to contribute—and they, in turn, would inspire even more people."*

Introduction

To our amazement, requests for more information ran over four times higher than for any previous series in *Sewing with Nancy's* 18-year history.

By early 1999, we had received over 20,000 mail, fax, phone and E-mail responses. Today we continue to process over 100 requests every week. Now in reruns, "Sew a Smile" continues to generate unprecedented viewer reaction.

**Contagious Generosity**

We were, and continue to be, deluged with reports of service projects. Some people copied the action plans in the series; others created their own or customized ours for a specific group. It soon became evident to me that handwork expertise was not a defining or limiting factor for the volunteers.

Surprisingly, many said they had little or no sewing know-how. Yet no matter what their talents, age, physical condition or gender, people were finding ways to organize, solicit, ship and create—all to serve others.

Their stories have convinced me, more than ever, that *Creative Kindness* is wonderfully contagious. As you read about the incredible dedication to helping in our world, you will reaffirm your own ability to make a difference.

In our cynical, too-busy and it's-your-problem culture, real people are somehow finding the hours and mustering the resources to help humanity, if only one project—or person—at a time.

***Creative Kindness* Takes Shape**

To help put a practical and insightful book together, I called on my good friend and well-known sewing journalist Gail Brown. Besides her professional talents, I knew Gail was personally aligned with this assignment.

In a speech she gives to high school seniors, she reveals her belief in service: "Persevering through hard times and rising from self-doubt is made easier through the reminder that some person, some cause, needs us. Those needs of others hold hope for you and me, even in our darkest hours."

Another voice was instrumental in shaping this project. Nancy's Notions' talented writer, Merry Anderson, generously contributed her publishing experience, her words and her vision, and in doing so, opened our minds and our definition of *Creative Kindness*.

Gail, Merry and I have selected samples from the thousands of "Sew a Smile" responses to share on our page-by-page sidebars. The quiet, unrequited actions of these can-do volunteers speak loudly and eloquently of their credibility, commitment and joy.

Through the dozens of interviews and hours of research for "Sew a Smile", the three of us, too, feel as though we are part of this growing "kindness community".

**Hands to Hearts, with Hope**

When Helen Littrell of Klamath Falls, Oregon contacted me, ecstatic, because she'd donated 700 head coverings to cancer treatment centers, I was uplifted from the fatigue of seemingly endless meetings, script drafts and administrative duties.

Helen's kindness—and energy!—convinced me that I could reach out beyond my daily responsibilities to help another. That night I went home and, in honor of a friend who recently died of cancer, I made a ComfortCap (see page 24) to donate to our local hospital.

And, as we finish this book, both Gail and I have more caps in the works: Merry's sister, Diane, is now recovering from mastectomy surgery and undergoing chemotherapy, as is Gail's friend Diana. Truly, their caps will be our gifts of love, dignity and hope.

Be inspired by all the real people who taught us about *Creative Kindness*. We dedicate this book to them. Their formula is simple but powerful—from hands to hearts, with hope.

That formula is within your reach. They are making a difference, and you can, too. The people and projects are here to show you how.

*Creative Kindness*…your life, and the lives of countless others, will never be the same.
—*Nancy Zieman*

*"In our cynical, too-busy and it's-your-problem culture, real people are somehow finding the hours and mustering the resources to help humanity, if only one project— or person—at a time."*

Newborn
in
Need

"caring for God's children"

**"Newborns in Need**
is an all-volunteer, organization. We have no corporate
or government sponsors or
funding. All items Newborns
in Need donates are free of
any charge."

I watch "Sewing with
Nancy" on T.V. and saw the
"Sew a Smile" series. I
was so moved by the
stories that I've decided
to start sewing with a
group of teenage girls.
We plan to make
baby blankets, bonnets
and kimonos for our
local hospitals neonatal
unit. We'll soon be
getting started with
our new group which
we're calling "Special Delivery."
Bev
Middletown, Ohio

# Little Needs, Big Hearts

## Infants Inspire Creative Kindness

IT WAS EASY to choose the cause to start our book with. Babies—especially needy babies—generate a universal response. No matter what the odds, we must, and will, feed, clothe and comfort these children.

It was also easy to be genuinely touched by the passionate people who serve fragile infants and their families. Their commitment usually means beyond-the-call-of-duty hours and energy.

But if you ask any of these dedicated volunteers, "Is it all worth it?" they will answer, in some form, "Yes. Caring for new lives renews my joy, my fulfillment and my life."

*"If I can stop one heart from breaking, I shall not live in vain."*
Emily Dickinson

# Friends of Mothers and Infants
## Jan Brostek: Putting Pins & Needles to Work

*Making a difference at Pins & Needles: Enthusiastic volunteers gather to sew, serve and share.*

"WHEN we first got involved with this project, we thought we would be helping babies," reports Jan Brostek, co-owner of the Pins & Needles Sewing Centers in Cleveland, Ohio. "Now we know *they help all of us*."

In response to a 1996 request by MetroHealth's "Friends of Mothers and Infants" program, Pins & Needles coordinated production of items for underprivileged babies and their families.

Little did Jan know then that her customers' donations of handmade T-shirts, booties, bibs, buntings and hats would total in the tens of thousands.

Donations and inquiries about how to set up similar groups came in from across the country, especially since Pins & Needles was featured on my *Sewing with Nancy* TV show. "We're always amazed to see what cute baby items are sent to us," says Jan.

Although Jan adds that "90% of the sewing is finished at home," the meetings for the Pins & Needles "Sewing for Babies" Club continue to bustle. Those who don't have the time or skills to sew or knit often donate materials so others can.

The program has provided many benefits for volunteers such as Shirley Tisher. "I suppose, like everyone else in the club, I started because I wanted to help," she says. "But, after donating items, I find I have gained much more than I have given. It aroused my creativity. I started making buntings and now love to quilt.

"If I can make one baby warm and comfortable, and one mother smile and feel proud because she knows someone thinks her baby's special, then I know I'm making a difference."

# Labors of Love
## Eunice Sprung: The "Sew Special Lady"

AFTER losing an eye to cancer, Eunice Sprung knew her outdoor activities on their Corona, South Dakota farm would be limited. A devout Christian, she "...asked the Lord if I could still be able to sew, and maybe I could do something to serve Him."

A friend shared an article about the need for volunteers to sew for preemies. "What an answer I received from the Lord," says Eunice. In September 1992, she shipped her first layettes to hospitals in St. Paul and Minneapolis—and "Sew Special" was born.

Since then, Eunice's passion for philanthropy has led to a growing "Sew Special Family" of volunteers, from 4-H groups to an assisted-living home.

Eunice estimates that she now relies on close to 40 active home sewers. Her own weekly commitment of office duties, speaking engagements and "working (sewing) days" hovers near full-time.

The collective dedication of her Sew Special Family has yielded nearly 33,000 "Labor of Love" projects (as Eunice calls them) in just 7 years—undershirts, sleepers, blankets, quilts, afghans and more—for hospitals, social services and community centers serving infants and young children.

Eunice's group invites ready-made donations, too—especially undershirts. She notes, "I will accept anything that will help me help others."

It isn't surprising that as the founder, chief organizer and fund-raiser, Eunice "doesn't get much time for sewing now." But she's still a hands-on contributor, assembling projects, sorting, cleaning, packing and delivering.

Despite diminished eyesight, an exhaustive schedule and requests for

*Newborn twins model the "Labors of Love" they received from Sew Special founder Eunice Sprung.*

more Labor of Love projects, Eunice remains steadfastly devoted to her calling—the needs of children.

## One Baby, One Person at a Time…
### Carol Green and Newborns in Need

CAROL GREEN, founder of Newborns in Need, knows firsthand that in helping others, we help ourselves.

"The person who has benefited the most from this work is me," she admits. "Through service, hearts are healed, pain is lessened and proper perspective on life is maintained.

"When I lost three children through miscarriage, I thought I would never survive emotionally. I did. Now I have the ability to help other mothers."

Carol's own hospital experiences showed her a heartbreaking reality—many babies are born into families who don't have adequate clothing or blankets—but they also led her to a solution.

To help solve the problem, she decided to make baby layettes, blankets and quilts…and recruit others to help.

Since then, both Carol's family—she and her husband, Richard, now have six children—and her "solution" have grown. Thousands of people are currently involved in the national network of Newborns in Need.

Chapters are diverse. One affiliate is the Preston Youth Correctional Facility in Ione, California (see page 79). Some carry a nickname of their own, such as the "Bag Ladies of Pocono Farms" in Pennsylvania, who help Ozark Mountain families.

Like Carol, many of her recruits

*Carol Green (left) takes a hands-on approach to directing Newborns in Need and helping babies.*

*"There was a 'Sew a Smile' segment called 'Sew Special' about a group that donated items for preemies. They wanted flannel and yarn for little caps. I have a little flannel I could use to make preemie outfits. The husband of a friend who died also gave me about 60 partial skeins of yarn that would be just enough for baby caps. I like to knit when I'm watching TV, and the caps could either be sent to the charity or donated to our local hospital."*

Rose
Nixa, Missouri

contribute to ease personal pain. "Maybe they have lost a child or grandchild," she says. "Maybe they can't have children. These are some of our greatest volunteers."

Her charity's newest projects-in-progress include the group's recent retail-store opening of "Little Darlins" next to the Newborns in Need national offices in Houston, Missouri.

Sponsorships from companies like Lee Middleton dollmakers have helped ease funding burdens, as have contributions by Fabric.com and other vendors. Carol still welcomes donations from individuals, too.

Carol's sights for Newborns in Need are set high. "I would like to see Newborns in Need—or a similar charity—in every major U.S. city. One person at a time, one baby at a time, we can make this world a better place."

# How You Can Quickly Assemble
## Our Creative Kindness Baby Layette

With a small investment of time and fabric, you can make a big difference in the lives of a family and their new child. This fast-to-finish, four-piece layette includes a sleeper, T-shirt, pants and receiving blanket that can either be sewn or serged.

### Supplies for One Layette

- *Creative Kindness* Layette patterns (included in this book—see pages 15-17 and page 20).

- **Materials needed for each item:**

    **T-shirt**—3/8 yd. (0.35 m) 58"-60" (147.5 cm-152.5 cm) cotton knit fabric, 3" x 26" (7.5 cm x 66 cm) ribbing.

    **Sleeper**—3/4 yd. (0.7 m) 58"-60" (147.5 cm-152.5 cm) cotton knit fabric, 3" x 26" (7.5 cm x 66 cm) ribbing, 12" (30.5 cm) lightweight zipper.

    **Pants**—1/2 yd. (0.5 m) 58"-60" (147.5 cm-152.5 cm) cotton knit fabric, 3" x 14" (7.5 cm x 35.5 cm) ribbing, 1/2 yd. 1/4" elastic.

    **Receiving blanket**—45" (115 cm) squares of two coordinating cotton flannel fabrics.

- **Matching all-purpose thread.**

- **Handy notions/equipment**—water-erasable marking pen or pencil; 1/4" quilting foot.

### Preparations

- Prewash the fabrics. Avoid using fabric softeners—a newborn's skin may be sensitive to softening agents.

- Photocopy to enlarge all the patterns. For small, medium and large sizes, enlarge 200%. For preemie sizes, enlarge the large size 150%. Cut out the pattern pieces.

- Select the correct size. Use these comparatives to ready-made sizes: preemie (preemie), small (0-3 months), medium (3-6 months) and large (6-9 months).

*"I learned that many babies in a certain region are born to mothers who have no prenatal care. After birth, the babies literally have nothing to wear home. This convinced me that our group, 'Tiny Stitches', was 'meant to be' and that even though we had no financial support at that time, we would make a difference in the babies' lives. Now we provide basic layettes that include sewn, knitted and crocheted items made by members."*

Sandra
Suwanee, Georgia

# Creative Kindness Baby Layette:
## Four Simple Projects to Completion

## Project 1:
## T-shirt

### Step 1: Cut and mark pieces.

- Cut out the front, a back and two sleeves (see #1 on page 14).

- Measure and cut 3" (7.5 cm) wide ribbing according to the chart below.

- Mark the sleeve and armhole notches, center front and center back using a fabric marking pen or pencil.

### Step 2: Add sleeves.

- Stitch or serge the sleeve front to the T-shirt front, right sides together, matching notches.

  **Note:** All patterns include 1/4" (0.6 cm) seam allowances. Stitch a straight seam and then zigzag the edges together. Or use a serger with a 4-thread overlock stitch. (Consider using a softer thread, such as Wooly Nylon, in the serger loopers.)

- Stitch or serge the sleeve back to the *(Instructions continue on next page)*

| | Preemie | Small | Medium | Large |
|---|---|---|---|---|
| Neckline | 10" (25 cm) | 11" (28 cm) | 12" (30.5 cm) | 13" (33 cm) |
| Long sleeve, cut 2 | 3" (7.5 cm) | 4" (10 cm) | 4-1/2" (11.5 cm) | 5" (12.5 cm) |
| Short sleeve, cut 2 | 3-3/4" (8 cm) | 4-3/4" (12 cm) | 5-1/4" (13.1 cm) | 5-3/4" (14.5 cm) |

Little Needs, Big Hearts

T-shirt back, right sides together, matching notches.

## Step 3: Apply the neckline ribbing.

- Join the short ends of the ribbing, right sides together, with a 1/4" (0.6 cm) seam. Finger-press the seam open.
- Fold band in half, meeting cut edges.

- Quarter-mark the band with pins, using seam as one quarter mark.
- Quarter-mark the neckline, using center front and back as two of the quarter marks.
- Meet the quarter marks of neckline and the band, right sides together. Pin. Stretch the ribbing to fit the neckline. Stitch or serge the band to the neckline.

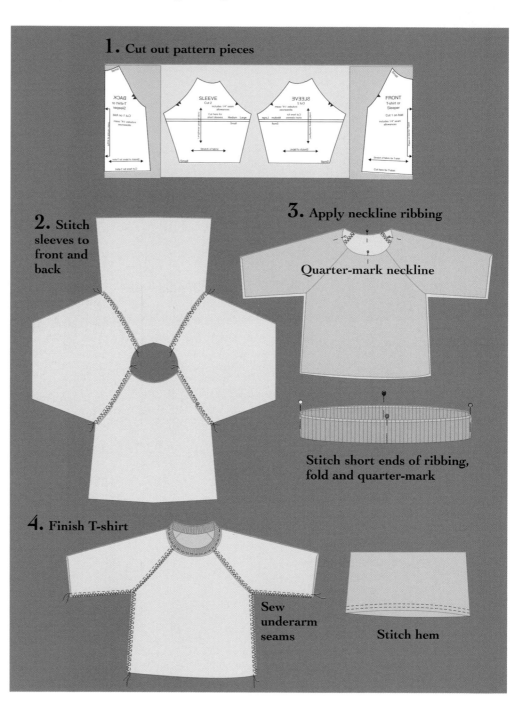

1. **Cut out pattern pieces**

2. **Stitch sleeves to front and back**

3. **Apply neckline ribbing**

**Quarter-mark neckline**

**Stitch short ends of ribbing, fold and quarter-mark**

4. **Finish T-shirt**

**Sew underarm seams**

**Stitch hem**

Little Needs, Big Hearts

## Step 4: Finish T-shirt.

- Meet the front and back, right sides together. Stitch or serge the side and underarm seams, matching the armhole seam.

- Sew the ribbing to the sleeves, following the same steps listed for the neckline ribbing.

- Stitch the T-shirt hem by folding up 3/4" (2 cm) hem on lower edge. Press. Topstitch the hem. *(Instructions continue on next page)*

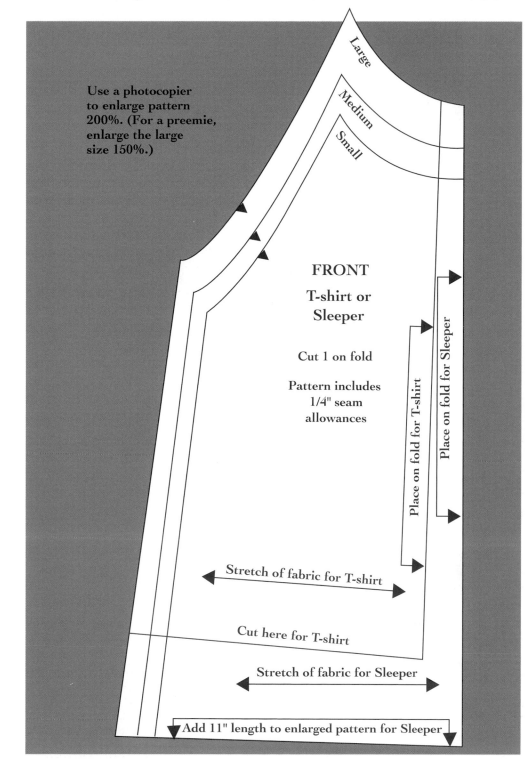

Use a photocopier to enlarge pattern 200%. (For a preemie, enlarge the large size 150%.)

Large

Medium

Small

**FRONT**

**T-shirt or Sleeper**

Cut 1 on fold

Pattern includes 1/4" seam allowances

Place on fold for T-shirt

Place on fold for Sleeper

Stretch of fabric for T-shirt

Cut here for T-shirt

Stretch of fabric for Sleeper

Add 11" length to enlarged pattern for Sleeper

*"We have been creating baby quilts for Pregnancy Helpline for several years. This year, we decided to give something back to the senior members who supported our parish for so many years. We found the need was much greater than expected—the 'visiting' outreach minister said she could 'get by' with 90 quilts for the sick, shut-in and needy."*

Sheryl
Janesville, Wisconsin

Little Needs, Big Hearts

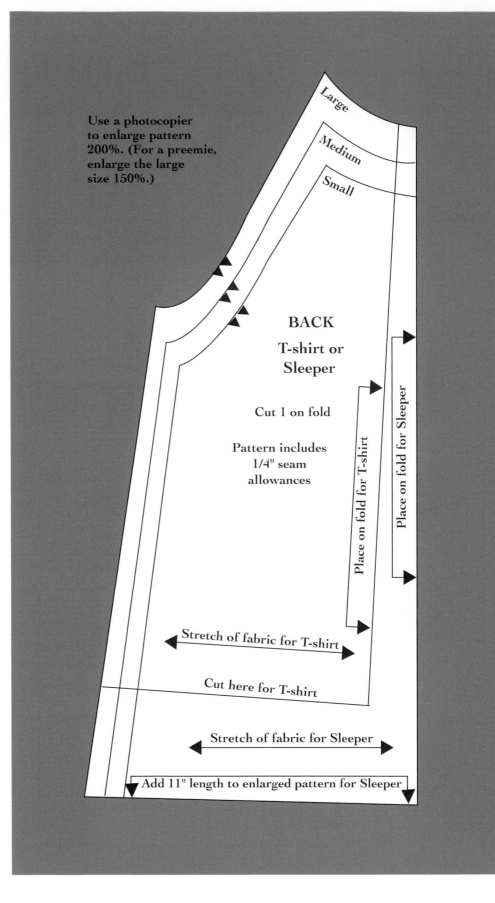

*"As of late, my little grandnephew was in the Primary Children's Medical Hospital in Salt Lake City with a heart condition. While there, my sister and niece took special notice of the shortage of all baby items. Sometimes it takes a mountain to fall on me! Then I thought of your 'Sew a Smile' series. I was delighted to return home and ask some others to help me sew projects for this hospital. Hopefully, I will make a tiny difference."*

Kim
Plain City, Utah

Use a photocopier to enlarge pattern 200%. (For a preemie, enlarge the large size 150%.)

Large

Medium

Small

BACK
T-shirt or
Sleeper

Cut 1 on fold

Pattern includes 1/4" seam allowances

Place on fold for T-shirt

Place on fold for Sleeper

Stretch of fabric for T-shirt

Cut here for T-shirt

Stretch of fabric for Sleeper

Add 11" length to enlarged pattern for Sleeper

Little Needs, Big Hearts

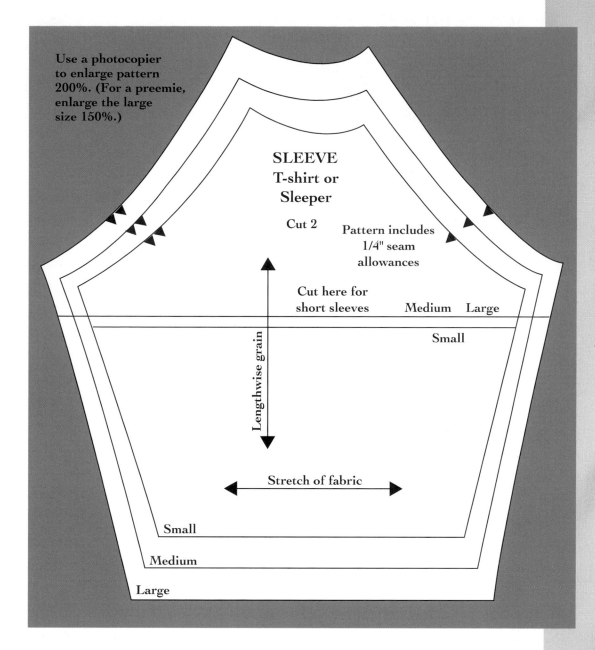

Use a photocopier to enlarge pattern 200%. (For a preemie, enlarge the large size 150%.)

**SLEEVE**
**T-shirt or Sleeper**

Cut 2

Pattern includes 1/4" seam allowances

Cut here for short sleeves

Medium    Large

Small

Lengthwise grain

Stretch of fabric

Small

Medium

Large

## *Project 2:* Sleeper

### Step 1: Cut and mark pieces.

- To make the sleeper pattern, lengthen the T-shirt front and back patterns 11". Cut out the back, a front and two sleeves.

- Mark center front for the zipper, measuring 12" (30.5 cm) from neckline. Stitch 1/4" (0.6 cm) on each side of marking (see #1 on page 18).

### Step 2: Insert zipper.

- Center lower edge of zipper, right side down, at lower edge of marking. Stitch across bottom of zipper, following reinforcement stitching.

- Cut along the center front, clipping diagonally into corners. Be careful not to clip the stitching.

- Fold the zipper up toward the neckline. Tuck under the center front allowances of the sleeper along stitching lines. Topstitch the zipper in *(Instructions continue on next page)*

Little Needs, Big Hearts

place. (For the easiest, straightest stitching, use a zipper foot.)

## Step 3: Assemble the pieces.

- Join the sleeves to the sleeper as for the T-shirt.

- Do not join the ends of the neckline ribbing. Fold the ribbing in half, meeting the lengthwise edges. Stitch curved seams at each end of the ribbing as shown in #3 below.

- Turn the ribbing right side out.

- Quarter-mark the neckline and rib-

bing. Meet the curved ends of the ribbing to the zipper edges. Meet the remaining quarter marks; attach and topstitch the ribbing as for the T-shirt.

- Meet the front and back pieces, right sides together. Stitch or serge the side and underarm seams, matching armhole seam.

- Stitch or serge the ribbing to sleeves same as for T-shirt.

- Stitch or serge the front and back together at lower edge. Turn the sleeper right side out.

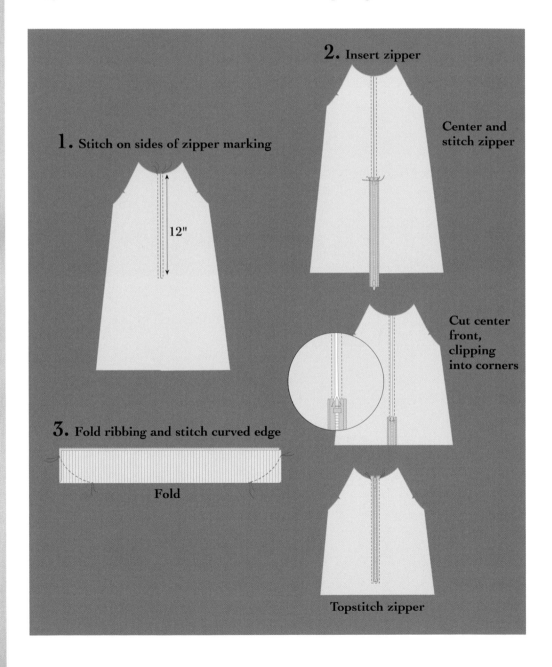

**1.** Stitch on sides of zipper marking

12"

**2.** Insert zipper

Center and stitch zipper

Cut center front, clipping into corners

**3.** Fold ribbing and stitch curved edge

Fold

Topstitch zipper

Little Needs, Big Hearts

# Project 3: Pants

## Step 1: Cut and mark pieces.

- Cut out two pant pieces. Also cut 3" (7.5 cm) ribbing and 1/4" (0.6 cm) elastic according to the chart below.

- Mark the top of pants with a fabric marker.

## Step 2: Stitch seams.

- Meet the inseam of each pant leg, right sides together. Stitch or serge.

- Prepare and apply the ribbing to the pant legs as for T-shirt.

- Slip one leg inside other, meeting right sides. Stitch or serge crotch seam, stopping 1/2" from top of center back. Advance thread and stitch final 1/8" (0.3 cm) of seam. This provides an opening for inserting elastic.

## Step 3: Create the elastic casing.

- Press under a 1/2" (1.3 cm) casing at top edge. Stitch close to the lower edge of casing.

- Zigzag one end of the elastic to a sturdy fabric scrap. Thread the elastic through the casing using safety pin or Bodkin.

- Butt the ends of the elastic; zigzag. Trim away excess elastic.

*(Instructions continue on next page)*

| | Preemie | Small | Medium | Large |
|---|---|---|---|---|
| Leg ribbing, cut 2 | 4" (10 cm) | 5-1/4" (13.1 cm) | 5-3/4" (14.5 cm) | 6-1/4" (15.6 cm) |
| Elastic | 12" (30 cm) | 14" (35.5 cm) | 15-1/2" (39.3 cm) | 17" (43 cm) |

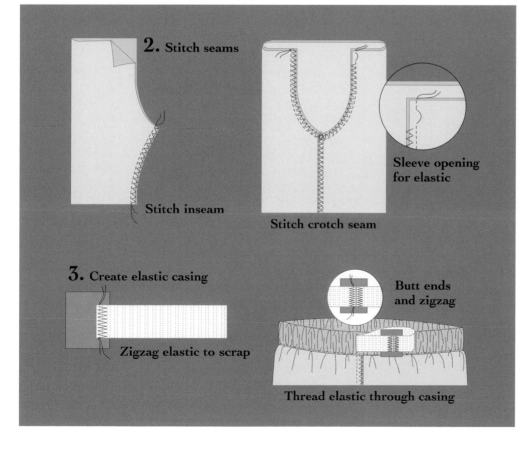

**2.** Stitch seams

Stitch inseam

Stitch crotch seam

Sleeve opening for elastic

**3.** Create elastic casing

Zigzag elastic to scrap

Butt ends and zigzag

Thread elastic through casing

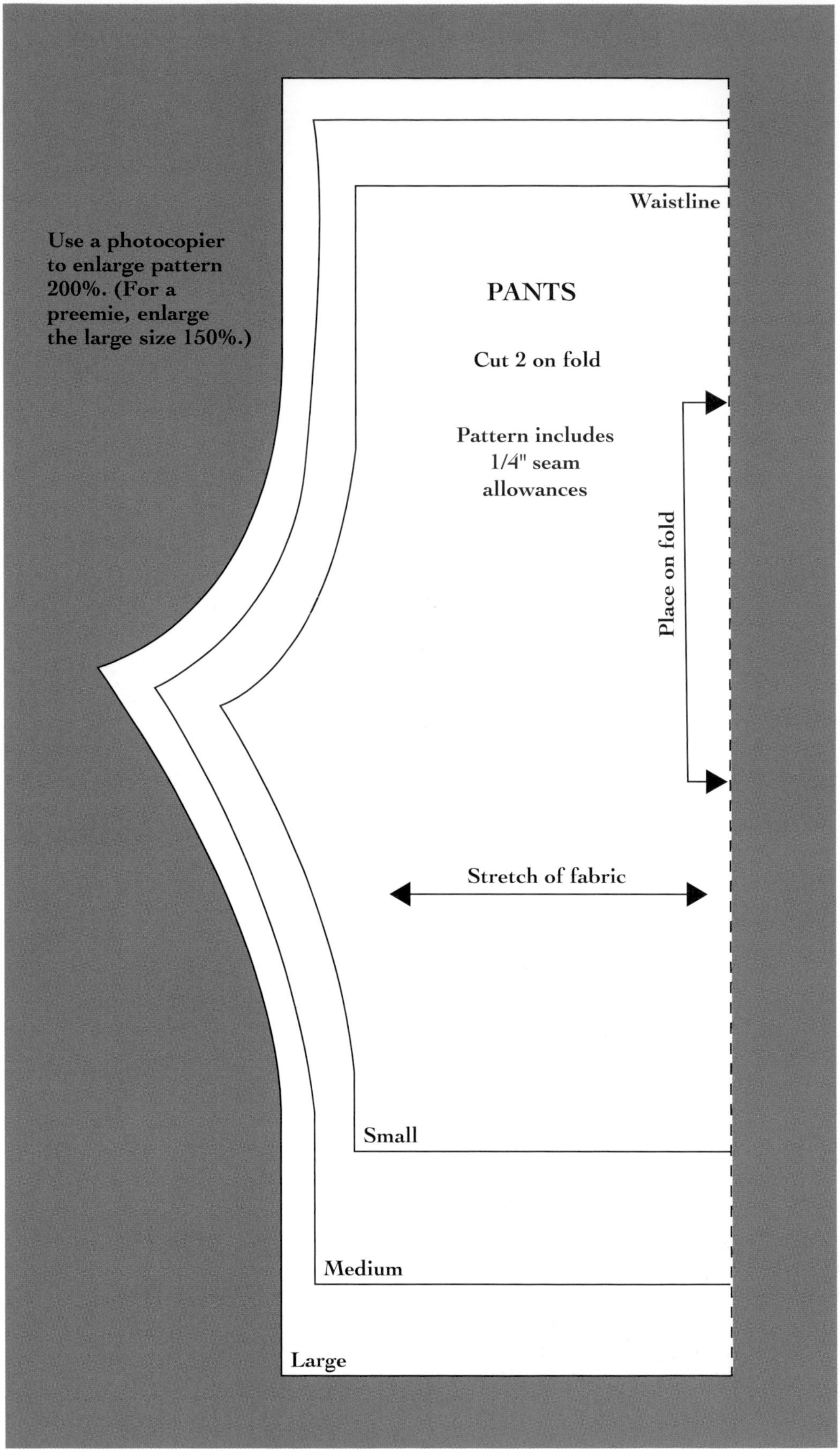

Use a photocopier
to enlarge pattern
200%. (For a
preemie, enlarge
the large size 150%.)

Waistline

## PANTS

Cut 2 on fold

Pattern includes
1/4" seam
allowances

Place on fold

Stretch of fabric

Small

Medium

Large

*"I was so excited about
making baby things
that I've started sewing
already! Please send
me a list of
charities in need of
'Sew a Smile' projects."*

Lilias
Portland, Oregon

Little Needs, Big Hearts

# Project 4:
# Receving Blanket

## Step 1: Cut pieces.

- Cut two 45" (115 cm) squares of fabric. (Cotton flannel is a good choice.)

## Step 2: Sew or serge seams.

- To sew the blanket, meet *right* sides together. Stitch around the outer edges using "wrapped" corners.

- Straight stitch a 1/4" (0.6 cm) seam along one edge of the blanket, sewing from edge to edge.

- Fold the seam along the stitching line. The seam allowance will "wrap" toward the inside of the blanket.

- Beginning at the fold, stitch a 1/4" (0.6 cm) seam along the next edge. This makes a wrapped corner.

- Repeat, wrapping and stitching each of the corners in sequence, leaving a 5"-6" (12.5 cm-15 cm) opening on the final side for turning.

- Turn the blanket right side out and stitch the opening closed. *Optional:* Topstitch the edges.

- To serge the blanket, meet *wrong* sides together. Serge around the outer edges, using a 3- or 3/4-thread overlock stitch. *Optional:* Use soft, decorative thread, such as Woolly Nylon, in the looper(s). Before serging, avoid slippage by machine basting the two layers together.

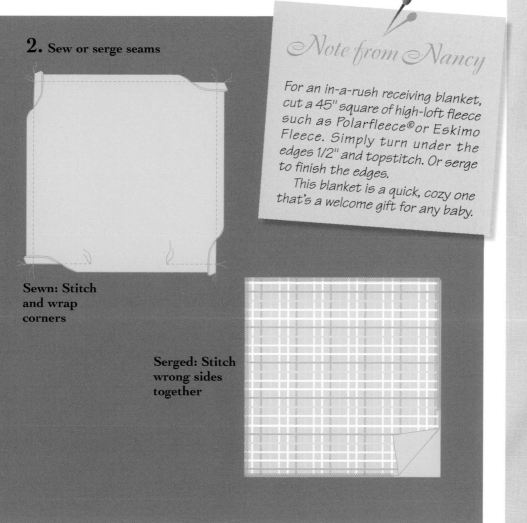

**2. Sew or serge seams**

**Sewn: Stitch and wrap corners**

**Serged: Stitch wrong sides together**

## Note from Nancy

For an in-a-rush receiving blanket, cut a 45" square of high-loft fleece such as Polarfleece® or Eskimo Fleece. Simply turn under the edges 1/2" and topstitch. Or serge to finish the edges.

This blanket is a quick, cozy one that's a welcome gift for any baby.

*"At St. Mary's Hospital here in Rogers, I understand that some newborns arrive with no baby clothes and are in need of something to go home in. I'm sure I would be able to sew a blanket like what was shown on your program."*

Willa
Rogers, Arizona

Little Needs, Big Hearts

Dear Nancy,
In the new issue of
Crafting Traditions magazine
you have an article called
"Crafting from the Heart".
I was unable to see the
3 part series called "Sew a
Smile" and I do not have a
computer. So would you
please send me the
information you talk about
in your article?
I have just lost my
husband because of a
brain tumor so I
thought maybe I could
help someone else.

Dorothy,
McComb, Ohio

Reach to Recovery

AMERICAN CANCER SOCIETY

FACTS ON BREAST CANCER

A visit...
pro...

comfortcap
Husqvarna VIKING
...ated especially for you by:

...aunder me with TLC. Har...
...n or machine wash on d...
...prefer mild soap

comfortca...
...sqvarna VIKIN...
...lly for you by:

...TLC. Hand

CREATIVE KINDNESS

# Gifts of Love, Dignity… And Hope

## ComfortCaps and Chemotherapy Turbans

THOUSANDS of *Sewing with Nancy* viewers wrote to me in response to our story about head coverings, telling how it inspired them into action.

Many of those letter writers were cancer survivors (…"I am at home recovering."). Or they had a daughter, sister, mother, aunt, friend or co-worker who had died or was suffering from this all-too-familiar disease.

Running through their messages was a common thread: In putting their hands and hearts to work helping others cope, they discovered healing—and hope.

Priced Sew Right
STAINLESS STEEL

"FOR my mother"… "for my sister"… "for my daughter"…"for my friend"…

I received more than 20,000 responses to my "Sew a Smile" series, many referring to the segment on chemotherapy head coverings.

Each letter was so personal and painful. Yet in each was also a determination not to let loved ones or memories surrender to despair.

Through their words, I met thousands of people—sufferers and their families and friends—who refused to let cancer control their lives. None could "fix" this disease, but all had resolved to do something proactive.

The "Sew a Smile" series featured a segment about the "Comfort Kerchief" (see page 25) head cover designed by Gaye Kriegel for her mother. Viewers responded by sending us other thoughtful and practical cap designs, along with their heart-tugging testimonials.

**More Than a Cap…**

Besides covering the heads of people who have lost hair due to chemotherapy, disease or trauma, these wig alternatives share another similarity: There never seem to be enough. No matter what the style, someone needs it and what it represents—encouragement and an emotional connection.

Bonnie Ellis and fellow Minnesota Quilt Guild member Mary Hess knew there was a need for head coverings— and hope. "Everybody knows somebody who hurts," says Bonnie.

This energetic duo began making ComfortCaps™ in the early 1990s. Bonnie explains that she has no power to say "no". "I guess I am one of those people who feel responsible," she says. She and Mary "wanted to do something for somebody with no strings attached."

Their lined cap was originally designed by a nun and cancer patient who found most hats hot and abrasive. The caps can consist of knit or woven fabric and feature a front brim for fullness.

*Made in minutes, "ComfortCaps" are attractive wig alternatives for those experiencing hair loss.*

Because seam allowances are hidden inside the lining, ComfortCaps are comfortable even when the wearer is lying down—which is important, because bald heads can get cold during sleep. Men like them, too, as a layer of warmth and softness under hats.

Easy to make "even on a treadle machine," the design is adaptable to decoration. Bonnie has seen ComfortCaps made with hand-marbleized fabric, adorned with metallic dots and machine-embroidered. The lining prevents trims from chafing the skin.

**A Caring Corporate Sponsor**

Bonnie and Mary's caps attracted the attention of Viking Sewing Machines, Inc., exclusive distributors of Husqvarna/Viking sewing machines. Nancy Jewell, Viking Publicity Director, was instrumental in setting up the grassroots ComfortCap sewing events throughout their dealer network.

Today, these events are ongoing and also include Comfort Pillows (see page 94) in various shapes and sizes.

When Viking adopted ComfortCaps as a corporate project, they sent Bon-

---

*"Please send me your head cover information. Less than a week ago, a very dear and longtime friend lost her life to cancer after a valiant fight. I would like to do more than make the customary donation."*

Judy
Seabrook, Texas

---

Gifts of Love, Dignity…and Hope

nie and Mary around the country to demonstrate cap construction and assembly-line production.

The caps have attracted audiences of all ages—"from 6 to 91," according to Mary. Even Bonnie's husband learned to make the cap and now joins in the teaching effort.

News of the easy-to-make, easy-to-wear design spread, and soon ComfortCaps were an international success.

Pattern requests have come in from all over Europe, and Bonnie and Mary have trained volunteers from Ecuador, Haiti, New Zealand, Australia and Canada. "Certainly," adds Bonnie, "cancer knows no boundaries."

### Caps Go to Work and Play

Today, doctors encourage chemotherapy patients to go about their lives as normally as possible. People "on chemo" are working, grocery shopping, watching a soccer game or mowing the lawn next door. This takes courage.

Hair loss can be a blow to a person's self-esteem. Women feel a loss of femininity, particularly if they are being treated for breast cancer and have had a mastectomy.

Knowing what to say or how to act can be awkward for all concerned, but getting involved in sewing ComfortCaps or any similar project can actually help break down those barriers.

Bonnie has seen this firsthand. "When you give something to someone," she says, "you connect with their inner feelings." Whenever she participates in a cap-making event, there are lots of hugs, tears and laughter.

One special cap stands out in her memory. She was at a consumer show with Mary, teaching a hands-on "make-it and take-it" ComfortCap class for Viking. A family had heard about the caps on TV and came to the booth.

Bonnie had just finished an elegant black cap, which she dressed up with hand-sewn rhinestones for the mother.

"The father was so grateful," Bonnie remembers. "He told me that they had lost five of their 12 children to cancer. Now his wife had it, but she wanted to look nice for their daughter's wedding."

Mary can't forget another special couple. Each sat at machine to make caps, and the husband began telling Mary how he felt about his wife's cancer, disclosing feelings he, regretfully, had not been able to discuss with her.

They all cried together, and the husband and wife walked off hand in hand.

### These Coverings Are Contagious!

On the "Sew a Smile" show, I reported Barb Prihoda's Lake Sewing Retreat. Barb, a well-known machine embroiderer, received a Comfort Kerchief from Gaye Kriegel while going through chemotherapy.

"Gaye's generosity and kindness were very touching," Barb remembers. "Her gift inspired me to return that kindness to others."

At her annual retreat, Barb proposed devoting one evening to cancer awareness and sewing head coverings. Everyone gladly agreed. Consistent with the ratios for middle-aged women, four of the 18 women there were cancer survivors.

With each head covering sewn and cancer story shared, all contributors felt a contagious spirit—an empowering sense of purpose and diminishing feelings of helplessness.

The "Sew a Smile" segment also inspired letter writers who had under-

*"These are more than just hats. They are hope. They connect people to each other in a unique way, to say 'I care' and to give patients a reason to live for today."*

Linda
Cleveland, Ohio

*At her annual Lake Sewing Retreat, well-known machine embroiderer Barb Prihoda and 17 friends gathered to share their sewing skills — and a collective spirit of purpose and kindness.*

Gifts of Love, Dignity…and Hope

gone brain surgery and bone marrow transplants, as well as sufferers of head-trauma accidents, Hodgkin's disease, scleroderma and other diseases. They all wanted instructions for making head coverings.

But weren't these the people who should be *receiving* head coverings, not making them?

Gail and I soon learned that the people suffering from life-threatening conditions are often those most eager to help others. Their way of fighting is to turn helplessness into purpose and isolation into companionship. Besides, there are no better authorities for design testing and improvement.

Bonnie recalls a seriously ill cancer patient who was making ComfortCaps. The woman didn't know how much longer she could use them but was certain there were others who could. It is people like this who teach us that *Creative Kindness* is really *Creative Courage*.

## Finding Volunteers and Getting Organized

Consider recruiting a group that meets for reasons other than sewing, such as for church, school, sport, business, civic or senior activities. With a little encouragement and guidance, everyone in the group—including non- and inactive sewers—can gain the confidence to take on ComfortCap-making.

For instance, no sewing skills are required for cutting out the patterns and fabric. Obviously, sewing, quilting and needleworking groups won't need much convincing—just a plan.

● Discuss who will receive your completed projects. Treatment centers, hospitals and nursing homes are all in need of alternative head coverings. Or perhaps you or your volunteers have friends or relatives who are or will be in need of caps.

● If your group doesn't have a regular meeting place for sewing, quilting or crafting, check out possible locations to hold this event.

Look into church fellowship rooms, community centers or sewing machine

dealerships. Many civic-minded organizations allow free use of space for volunteer events.

● Depending on the life- and work-styles of volunteers, choose a morning, afternoon or early evening session of 2 to 3 hours. One individual can easily make two caps in an hour.

An "open house" format works well—volunteers on tight schedules can come in, complete one cap and leave feeling like they have made a tangible contribution.

● Ask each volunteer to read through the "Supplies for One ComfortCap" and "Preparations" lists (see page 27) and to bring enough materials for at least two caps.

● Have those easy-to-overlook items on hand: extra patterns, extension cords, power strips, extra irons and ironing surfaces, extra cutting and marking tools and bags for finished caps.

● Create a comfortable atmosphere. Request that one or two volunteers bring favorite snacks and beverages.

*Note from Nancy*

Keep in mind that your "group" can be just one person—you. Don't let our tips for organizing volunteers discourage you from a solo effort.

● To stage a productive event, make step-by-step samples of the project beforehand. If you don't have time, photocopy the "Five Simple Steps to Completion" on page 28, enlarging if desired. Post the samples or photocopies on a bulletin board or wall.

● Use the gathering as an opportunity to build awareness of cancer risk factors and the need for regular personal and professional exams.

● Assign volunteers to deliver the caps to your charity of choice. Or volunteers can take caps to individuals they know are in need. Package each cap in a bag and label it with the tag found inside the ComfortCap pattern.

● Keep in mind that the need is ongoing and constant. Bonnie and Mary suggest asking participants to make cap pledges for the next year.

## How You Can Quickly Assemble
## A ComfortCap

The step-by-step assembly and sewing tips that we provide here will help streamline construction of the ComfortCap. However, a pattern for the project is not included in this book. Patterns are available from local authorized Husqvarna/Viking dealers.

To find a dealer near you, check the Yellow Pages or call 1-800/358-0001. Dealers are also listed on the Web site www.husqvarnaviking.com.

**If you make the cap(s):** This cap is the epitome of ease. You can complete one effortlessly in 20 minutes.

**If your group makes the caps(s):** Because of the simplicity of the cap's construction, dividing duties among participants is also simple. One group can cut and one group can sew.

### Supplies for
### One ComfortCap

● **ComfortCap pattern (available from local authorized Husqvarna/Viking dealers—see above).**

● **Soft cotton knits or lightweight cotton fabrics.** When worn, the cap will be turned back, exposing the lining. When choosing a lining fabric, use the same fabric as the outer cap or use a soft coordinating one.
The following are the yardage requirements per cap:

Adult: 1/2 yd. (60" wide) knit fabric
3/4 yd. (45" wide) woven fabric

Child: 1/3 yd. (60" wide) knit fabric
5/8 yd. (45" wide) woven fabric

● **Matching all-purpose thread.**

### Note from Nancy

Bonnie Ellis recommends against using black (unless for a special occasion) or yellow fabric, because these colors can be unflattering to the changed skin tones of those undergoing chemotherapy.

### Preparations

● To minimize shrinkage and dye rub-off, pre-wash and dry fabrics.

● Color-coordinate the fabric and lining of two (or more) caps so that they can be sewn simultaneously without re-threading your sewing machine.

● Follow the guidesheet instructions for preparing the caps and lining patterns as well as for stitching the caps. Then, to streamline assembly, divide the construction into five main steps as described on page 28.

### Note from Nancy

I love sergers, but I don't recommend using them for your cap. Serged seams are bulkier and could possibly be irritating to sensitive skin, as can lace edgings, trims, buttons, hooks or elastics.

*"I am very interested in making caps for the local cancer center. I have time on my hands as I am at home recovering from ovarian cancer. People have been so kind to me during this difficult time in my life. I think making caps will be a way I can give back to the cancer center that has been very supportive. As a cancer survivor, I really appreciate all you have done to help people feel better about themselves."*

Marlene
Canal Fulton, Ohio

Gifts of Love, Dignity…and Hope

# ComfortCap:
# Five Simple Steps to Completion

## Step 1: Cut out the fabric.

- To save time and yardage, cut out two or more ComfortCaps at the same time. Stack two folded layers of fabric and pin the pattern pieces through all layers. You'll need an outer cap and a lining cut from the same pattern.

  Cut knits on the grain (shown in #1 at right); cut wovens on the bias (not shown). Also consider using electric scissors or a rotary cutter and cutting mat for the fastest, cleanest cutting through the multiple layers.

## Step 2: Stitch the outside darts.

- Straight-stitch the two outside darts.

- Repeat on the lining piece.

## Step 3: Stitch the center back seam and third dart.

- Stitch the center back seam into the center dart.

- Repeat for the lining piece.

## Step 4: Stitch the cap and lining together.

- Place the cap and lining inside each other, right sides together.

- Stitch around the brim, leaving an opening for turning.

## Step 5: Finish the cap.

- Turn the cap right side out.

- Hand-stitch the opening closed.

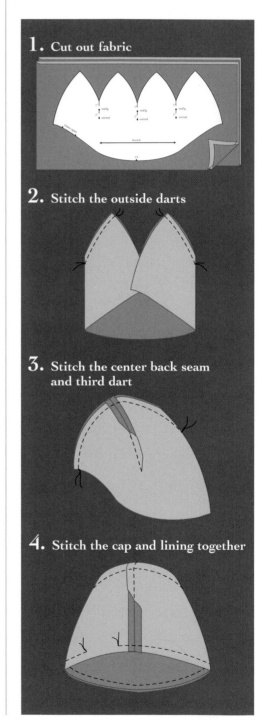

**1.** Cut out fabric

**2.** Stitch the outside darts

**3.** Stitch the center back seam and third dart

**4.** Stitch the cap and lining together

Gifts of Love, Dignity…and Hope

# Creative Kindness Continues
## The Reaction—and Actions

ONE PERSON, some fabric and thread and good intentions—it doesn't seem like an awful lot. Just how much difference can that make in someone's life? You might ask Helen Littrell of Klamath Falls, Oregon. That is, if you can find her and slow her down.

She may be "riding around in the boondocks in my pickup," as she tells it. In 1 year, from January 1999 to January 2000, Helen—entirely on her own—made over 700 Comfort Kerchiefs (see page 24) and donated them to cancer centers in her local area and beyond in southern Oregon.

### *Sewing with Nancy* Connection

Although retired, Helen is familiar with the hospital environment through her part-time work as a medical transcriptionist. She also sews clothes for premature infants and makes bereavement outfits, but she had not heard of Comfort Kerchiefs until she saw them on *Sewing with Nancy*.

Helen sent for the directions and made a few, but then went one step further. "I actually wore one around all day," she explains, "and then I made some revisions."

Like many of us, Helen had never experienced hair loss, and wearing the kerchief gave her a firsthand feeling for head coverings and some empathy for those who must wear them. She has seen baseball cap-type headwear but prefers making kerchiefs "because they're not as obvious."

Once she had stitched a few kerchiefs, Helen had to figure out what to do with them. She recommends putting together a list of local hospitals and cancer treatment centers, then calling the public relations director or office. From there, she is always directed to the right person or place.

### Hundreds of Needs

Helen creates Comfort Kerchiefs for people she will never meet. She has, however, heard from some of the peo-

*Helen Littrell single-handedly made more than 700 Comfort Kerchiefs—in just 1 year!—and gave them to thankful cancer patients in Klamath Falls and elsewhere in southern Oregon.*

ple who have benefitted from her handmade donations.

One letter, she recalls, was from a nurse. "The kerchiefs allow her to keep working while undergoing treatment," Helen says, "so I made her some extra white ones."

Because she has a limited income, Helen relies on donations and fabric sales to provide the materials for her kerchiefs. She has no intention of stopping production, despite the financial challenges she faces.

"I don't know why I'm driven to do it," she admits. "It's a compulsion." Helen may call it compulsion, but we simply call it *Creative Kindness*.

*"I am interested in receiving the 'Sew a Smile' listing. I am employed by a clinic as an oncology nurse clinician, administering chemotherapy to people with cancer. I am also an avid seamstress. I make many hats and turbans for the women who lose their hair from the treatments they receive. I wish you could see how good it makes these women feel to know that someone is thinking of them at a time when their self-image is threatened."*

Nancy
Marshfield, Wisconsin

Gifts of Love, Dignity…and Hope

COMFORT KERCHIEF designer Gaye Kriegel also referred us to Maryen Rogers of Searcy, Arkansas. Maryen and the members of the Bernina Sewing Club create unique head coverings of their own to give to cancer patients experiencing hair loss.

"The Chemotherapy Turban, as we call it, is so simple to make that 15 members of my sewing club completed 191 of them in a single day," says Maryen. "There are lots of turban patterns around, but our experiments have streamlined this one so that it can be mass-produced.

"It doesn't take much fabric or much sewing skill, so we encourage everyone we know to join together for this worthy cause."

Maryen and her fellow volunteers make the turban in three sizes, "mostly the medium size," Maryen notes. "The small size would fit a young teen." Each turban is packaged in a plastic bag with a printed note tucked inside. It states the size and that the turban was "Made for a Special Person".

Maryen adds, "I distribute the turbans to radiation treatment centers and oncologists. We suggest that each patient receive three turbans—one to wear, one to wash and a spare."

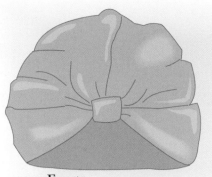

**Front**

**Side**

*Easy to make and wear, the Chemotherapy Turban (illustrated here) is another popular head covering.*

## How You Can Quickly Assemble
## Chemotherapy Turbans

**If you make the turban(s):** This turban requires minimal fabric, time and sewing skill, so you'll complete a number of them quickly. (Each step takes about 10 minutes, for a total of no more than 1 hour for each turban.)

**If your group makes the turban(s):** Use our simple five-step approach on page 31 to streamline your turban "manufacturing".

We recommend you set up the work area as a series of workstations, with each station specializing in one part of the process (for example, cutting, adding band, making tucks, etc.).

### Supplies for Two Turbans

- **3/8-1/2 yd. (0.34-0.46 m) stretch knit fabric 60" (152.4 cm) wide.** (More cotton in the blend provides more coolness and less slippage.)

- **Matching all-purpose thread.**

- **Basic notions/equipment**—zigzag sewing machine, pins, scissors.

- **Handy notions/equipment**—serger sewing machine (to allow the quickest construction); rotary cutter, ruler and mat; matching upholstery or quilting thread; large-eye hand-sewing needle.

Gifts of Love, Dignity…and Hope

# Chemotherapy Turban:
# Five Simple Steps to Completion

## Step 1: Cut out the turbans.

- For efficiency, cut out two or more turbans at one time. (Medium is the most popular size.)

- Cut according to the chart below and Illustration #1 at right.

- All sizes use the same size tab.

- Use only stretch knits, cutting the pieces on the stretchiest (usually crosswise) grain.

## Step 2: Sew the band to the turban.

- Use 1/2" (1.3 cm) seam allowances throughout. To seam, zigzag with a wide, standard length stitch and trim to the stitching (or serge with a balanced, medium-to-wide stitch).

- Fold the band in half lengthwise, wrong sides together.

- Align raw edges with one long side of turban, right sides together. Stitch the seam.

## Step 3: Create turban back.

- Fold the banded turban piece in half, crosswise, right sides together.

- Sew or serge the seam, beginning at the banded edge, rounding off the back corner point and stopping 1" (2.5 cm) before reaching the front folded edge (see #3 at right). The tab will be inserted through this opening later.

- Secure the thread tails and turn the turban right side out.

## Step 4: Pleat turban back.

- Fold up and pin three pleats about 3/4" (1.9 cm) deep, perpendicular to the back seam allowance.

- Stitch in the ditch to secure the pleats. If the fabric is too thick to machine-stitch, hand-sew along the seam using a large needle and quilting thread.

## Step 5: Add the tab and front pleats.

- Fold tab in half lengthwise, right sides together; sew or serge the seam.

- Turn the tab right side out. Center the seam on the underside; press.

- Slip tab through opening in turban seam (see #5 below right).

- Fold up and stack the pleats along the front seam, from the lower band edge to the opening. These pleats are like those at the back except they are stacked and *not* stitched.

- Wrap the tab around the pleats and sew the tab ends, right sides together.

- Rotate tab seam to hide it under the turban; machine-tack to center front seam allowance, preventing any gap between.

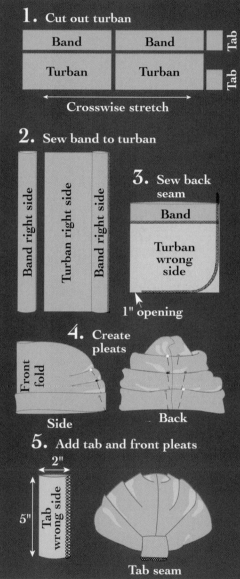

1. Cut out turban
Band  Band  Tab
Turban  Turban  Tab
Crosswise stretch

2. Sew band to turban
Band right side  Turban right side  Band right side

3. Sew back seam
Band
Turban wrong side
1" opening

4. Create pleats
Front fold
Side  Back

5. Add tab and front pleats
2"
5"  Tab wrong side
Tab seam

| Size | Turban | Band | Tab |
|------|--------|------|-----|
| Small | 20-1/2" x 8"<br>(52.3 x 20.5 cm) | 20-1/2" x 5"<br>(52.3 x 12.5 cm) | 5" x 4"<br>(12.5 x 10 cm) |
| Medium | 22" x 9"<br>(56 x 23 cm) | 22" x 5"<br>(56 x 12.5 cm) | 5" x 4"<br>(12.5 x 10 cm) |
| Large | 24" x 10"<br>(61 x 25.5 cm) | 24" x 5"<br>(61 x 12.5 cm) | 5" x 4"<br>(12.5 x 10 cm) |

I sew clothes for children and accessories for nursing home residents. I also make tablecloths and school bags for missions through my church. Besides being active, I enjoy doing sewing and to be crafting allow me to be of service to others. It makes me feel good to think my handiwork brings joy into other people's lives.

Vallie
Fayetteville, Arkansas

## CREATIVE KINDNESS

# One Person Can Make a Difference

### Enriching Others' Lives— And Our Own

IN a world full of seemingly insurmountable problems, how can one person make a difference?

It's easy to be skeptical. And sadly, our skepticism can paralyze us, preventing us from taking positive action.

We need to break away from this pessimism, to know that there are people who make a difference—and that we can, too.

The inspiring volunteers profiled in this chapter prove the incredible power of just one person. No matter how young, old, busy, budget-challenged or culturally divergent, these individuals have enriched thousands of lives—and in the process, their own.

# Creative Kindness
## Has No Age Requirement
### Molly Stanley and the Care Cloth Campaign

YOU'VE heard the stereotyping: "All teenagers want to do is have fun without responsibility." "Kids have no idea what the real world is like." "Young people just don't care." But 17-year-old Molly Stanley doesn't have time to worry about teenage typecasting.

She's too busy teaching sewing to elementary school students, finishing 4-H projects, working in youth volunteer organizations, designing and creating award-winning fashions, doing homework and making what brought this talented Arkansas teenager to our attention—"Care Cloths".

When Molly first saw my "Sew a Smile" series on *Sewing with Nancy*, she was inspired to start her own community project. She remembered speaking with a woman living in a shelter who

*Molly Stanley (left) makes creating Care Cloths a family event, with everyone gathered to help.*

said her most coveted item was her own bar of soap—one she didn't have to share.

### Creativity and a Washcloth…

Touched by this simple request, Molly's creative mind went to work. She took a plain washcloth, then folded it to form a pouch that could be filled with sample toiletries like soap,

toothpaste, shampoo and razors. Her "Care Cloth" campaign began.

Molly's 4-H group joined in on the project and started producing Care Cloths for her cause. Her beginning sewing class was also able to help, stitching the simple straight seams and putting on the ribbon ties. Consider the even greater lesson Molly was teaching her students—*Creative Kindness*.

Without a project budget, Molly had to rely on her resourcefulness when gathering materials. "The original supply of 20 washcloths came from my mother's 'recycling' trunk, where she stores things she purchased on sale in hopes of using them in a craft project," Molly explains.

### Next Challenge: Toiletries

"Local stores and civic clubs donated washcloths. Anyone and everyone donated the toiletries!" she laughs. "Whenever I teach a beginning sewing project, the kids have to bring toiletries as their 'dues' for the class."

When Molly's group attended 4-H counselor training, her fellow members gathered up bars of soap from the hotel rooms they stayed in and donated the bars. "Unfortunately, that was before any of us took a shower—so we really didn't smell too great by the end of the weekend," Molly laughs.

"A fraternity at a local college also put on a toiletry drive. And I am trying to get toothpaste donated by local dentists, because this is the most difficult—and expensive—thing to get."

One of the most touching and meaningful aspects of Molly's project is what she and her friends are learning about the recipients. When she first began making Care Cloths, Molly actually did not know what she was going to do with them.

"There is a home for troubled teens in our town," Molly explains. "They

One Person *Can* Make a Difference

ran an ad in the paper requesting hygiene products. I called them and told them about our Care Cloths, and they were thrilled. This was a great place to start, because it was for young people very similar to us."

**Care Cloths Discovered**

Word about the Care Cloths quickly spread to the director of the American Red Cross, who wanted to use them for disaster relief projects. Personnel at a battered women's shelter also heard about the project and took Molly, her family and friends on an eye-opening tour of the facilities.

"I think this was the most difficult place to visit," Molly admits. "My little brother had a lot of questions, so it gave my mom a great opportunity to teach us all about abuse, how to avoid it and how men should always respect women. It's been a learning process for everyone in our club."

The Care Cloth project continued to grow when the director of Bethlehem House, a homeless shelter in Molly's town, learned about it and asked for help. The resulting Bethlehem House Care Cloths are customized for men needing a shower and shave.

**Teens Make a Difference**

"I think," says Molly, "that one of the coolest things about all of this is that the community is really starting to see that people my age can—and will—make a difference if given a chance."

Molly didn't let her youth get in the way of making a difference. Remember her resolve if you find yourself saying "I'm too old", "I'm too young", "I can't sew (knit, crochet, quilt, coordinate, gather supplies, package or ship)", "I am disabled", "I would be the only person in my community doing this".

Remember it, too, if you find yourself making the most flawed assumption of all: "No one needs me." We guarantee—*someone does need you.*

Create some kindness and watch how quickly your initial hesitation is replaced with inspired action. And, as Molly shows, you can begin with a simple washcloth and bar of soap.

*Note from Nancy*

Would you like to help Molly and her Care Cloth campaign, or one of the other volunteers and charities in this book? Or, are you trying to locate notions we've listed?

Find all the information you need on our Creative Kindness Reference List, complete with names, phone numbers and street and Internet addresses. It's available on our Web site (www.creativekindness.com) and by mail (see page 94).

## How You Can Quickly Assemble
### Care Cloths

**If you make the cloth(s):** Incorporate 5- to 10-minute sewing sessions throughout your schedule, and you'll soon have a collection of Care Cloths to fill with toiletries and donate.

Each of the four steps (see page 36) will take about 5 minutes, for a total of about 20 minutes for each cloth. Finding time to complete one or two Care Cloths per week would be realistic even for the busiest volunteer.

**If your group makes the cloth(s):** Use our four-step approach on page 36 to streamline your "manufacturing". Each team can specialize in a certain step or steps. (Step order must be maintained so that Step 2 follows Step 1, Step 3 follows Step 2 and so on.)

Or, because this project is very simple and quick, each volunteer could make several complete Care Cloths.

*(Instructions start on next page)*

One Person *Can* Make a Difference

## Supplies for One Care Cloth

- **One standard washcloth.**

- **20" (51 cm) length of 1/4" (0.6 cm) washable satin or grosgrain ribbon** (to color-coordinate with the washcloth).

- **Matching all-purpose thread.**

- **Basic personal hygiene items**—toothbrush, disposable razor, small travel-size shampoo, toothpaste, facial soap, anti-bacterial hand wash, comb.

- **Basic notions/equipment**—sewing machine (any straight-stitch model or better), iron and ironing board, pins, scissors.

- **Handy notions**—Dritz Ezy-Hem® gauge (see "Note from Nancy" below), fabric marking pen.

*Helping others brings a smile, as Molly Stanley (standing at left), her family and friends show.*

# Care Cloth: Four Simple Steps to Completion

## Step 1: Form the pocket.

- Carefully remove the manufacturer's tag from the washcloth.

- Turn up lower edge of the washcloth 4" (10 cm) and finger-press (see #1 at upper right).

- Pin along both sides and the top edge of the pocket to prevent shifting.

## Step 2: Divide and mark the caddy into pockets.

- Fold ribbon in half; insert and pin

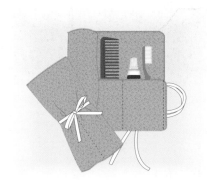

fold in right side seam 3-1/2" (9 cm) from lower edge, sandwiching ribbon between washcloth layers (see #2).

- Using a fabric marking pen, mark three pocket stitching lines from the upper edge to the fold as illustrated in #2.

## Step 3: Stitch the pockets.

- Set up the sewing machine for

*Note from Nancy*

The Dritz Ezy-Hem® gauge is the perfect aid for measuring and positioning washcloth pockets very quickly and accurately. (For shopping information, see page 94.)

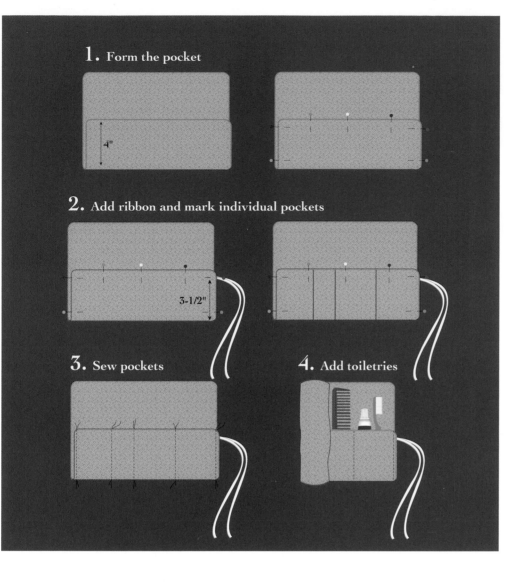

**1.** Form the pocket

4"

**2.** Add ribbon and mark individual pockets

3-1/2"

**3.** Sew pockets

**4.** Add toiletries

straight-stitching (10-12 stitches per inch).

- Stitch the sides with a 1/4" (0.6 cm) seam, catching the ribbon in the right side seam. For durability, be sure to back-stitch at both ends of all stitching.

- Stitch along the three marked lines to form four pockets (see #3).

- Remove the pins.

## Step 4: Fill the caddy.

- Fill the pockets with basic personal hygiene items.

- Roll or fold caddy from the left side to the right side. Wrap the ribbon

ties around Care Cloth and secure.

- Add a special touch with a note of hope and encouragement tucked under the ribbon tie.

*Note from Nancy*

Hotel toiletries are perfect fillers for Care Cloths. Contact friends who travel frequently and ask them to collect these hospitality give-aways. Or check with local hotels, inquiring about toiletry donations.

One Person *Can* Make a Difference

# Working Full-Time After Work
## Cheryl Henry and Sew Tiny Angels

"WHEN I retire, I plan on volunteering more."

One time or another, just about all of us have made that vow — if not aloud, then to ourselves. All of us, that is, except possibly Cheryl Henry of Columbus, Nebraska.

She isn't waiting for retirement. Despite a 40-hour workweek, this 53-year-old housekeeping supervisor squeezes in 2 to 4 hours — almost daily — to make "Sew Tiny Angel Quilts" for the University of Nebraska Neonatal Intensive Care Unit (NICU).

### Guardian Angel Quilts

Many in the University of Nebraska NICU believe that Cheryl's tireless spirit is passed on to these born-too-early babies. Since 1997, without exception, the "Sew Tiny Angels" who

*Cheryl Henry donates dozens of color-matched Sew Tiny Angel Quilt sets each year. Each one includes a quilt, sleeper, eye protector, hat and booties.*

*In her double-duty dining/sewing room, Cheryl Henry creates Angel Quilts in her hours after work. The quilts go to needy infants in her area.*

have been sent home with her anonymously donated quilts have thrived.

Those who work in the ward call the quilts, in keeping with their therapeutic record, "The Guardian Angels".

Coincidentally, Cheryl was a premature baby herself. Maybe that had

something to do with why she took a particular interest in the *Sewing with Nancy* "Sew a Smile" series and, more specifically, the segment on sewing for needy infants.

### The Need: Bereavement Outfits

Sometime later, her son, a funeral director in Omaha, asked her for a special favor: Could she make a bereavement outfit for a premature baby who had died?

Cheryl's work on this sensitive project showed her the difficulty of dressing tiny babies. There simply weren't any clothes proportioned to fit.

"What a terrible time for parents and families," Cheryl notes. "Then, these families cannot find clothes to fit the baby for burial. Children should look beautiful when sent to their heavenly home."

Thankfully, in this age of intensive-care medical technology, the need for infant bereavement outfits isn't frequent. But this situation awakened Cheryl to the unanswered layette needs of premature babies.

She called the University of Ne-

One Person *Can* Make a Difference

braska NICU and asked how she could help in other ways. "Sew Tiny Angel Quilts" were born.

**Low-Tech, High Production**

Despite her after-hours dedication to constructing these quilts, Cheryl's approach is very hands-on, low-tech and non-production-mode. Her only machine assistance is an early model Nelco sewing machine. In response to requests by the hospital staff, she uses her knitting skills as well.

For Cheryl, *Creative Kindness* is just that—an opportunity to share both creativity and kindness. She prides herself on the "ensembles"—sleeper, quilt, eye protector, hat and booties—each with customized color schemes and unique designs, crafted from fabric and yarn in her sewing room.

Of course, angels are a quilt-motif

*Note from Nancy*

If you'd like to help Cheryl Henry or any of the other individuals or groups in this book, you can consult our continually updated Creative Kindness Reference List.

Available on our Web site (www.creativekindness.com) and by mail (see page 94), the list includes complete contact information.

favorite, as are the whimsical bunnies, boats and ducks often featured on the carefully engineered quilts. To size down the matching sleepers, Cheryl starts with a 15-inch doll pattern, adapting the dimensions to fit a 4- to 5-pound baby.

Cheryl's state spirit is not forgotten, either. Nearby Lincoln is college football country, and for a baby born on a University of Nebraska game day, Cheryl created a special "Herbie Husker" ensemble.

She makes twin sets, too, and looks forward to the day when she'll need "threesome sets" for triplets.

Although Cheryl can always use donations of materials, such as batting, thread, flannel and juvenile prints, she never seems short on energy or on encouragement from her husband, Harold, and two grown children.

She produces at least 24 Angel Quilt ensembles a year, in addition to larger quilts donated for a variety of charitable projects. She also maintains her dedication to helping grieving families by providing infant bereavement outfits whenever needed.

**Charity = Energy**

Cheryl's do-it-now philosophy may inspire others to rethink their "I'll volunteer when I retire" mind-set. Her charity is her energy. She sums it up when she says, "I don't get tired. I can't wait to get home from work every day and get going on my Angel Quilts."

*Note from Nancy*

Both Gail and I were intrigued by Cheryl's "eye protector" story. Evidently, these 10" by 12" self-lined flannel rectangles shield sleeping infants' eyes from the brightly lit hospital isolettes.

While not being used by the baby, the protector is carried by the mother inside her clothing, close to her skin. Then, when the protector is put back on the baby's eyes, the mother's scent comforts and quiets the infant.

To make the eye protectors, Cheryl simply stitches together two 10" by 12" flannel rectangles, right sides together, leaving a 2" opening for turning. After turning right sides out, she presses and topstitches the edges.

Her 40" by 40" Angel Quilts are often used in the hospital, too. The blankets are draped over the isolettes, both for protection from the lights and for insulation.

*"I enjoy making items for preemies, cancer patients, children and elderly people. During the past several years I have made many items for hospitals and group homes, such as preemie gowns, hats and booties. I hand-sew all my items because it means so much more. I enjoy doing these things in my spare time, as I have a disabled husband who needs my attention also."*

Mary
Spencer, Indiana

One Person *Can* Make a Difference

# One-Woman Production, Production-Level Kindness
## Vallie Cole, Volunteer Extraordinaire

VOLUNTEERISM is part of Vallie Cole's everyday "to-do" list. As a *Northwest Arkansas Times'* headline stated, "This Busy Bee Member Lives Up to Name". Whether dressing dolls for the Salvation Army or sewing T-shirts for needy kids, the Fayetteville, Arkansas senior is seldom idle.

At one county fair alone, Vallie's entries included 27 clothing items, two quilts, several pot holders, pillows, tree ornaments, a sweater and vest and a braided rug—the majority of which were later donated to charity.

### Retired, Resourceful, Resilient

No doubt, some of this retired nurse's hands-on, can-do attitude comes from her upbringing. She was the firstborn of eight children. Her mother was too busy with other family members to teach her sewing, so she learned from a neighbor and in

*"Today my friend and I watched your show with excitement and agreed that there was a reason we were both able to see it. We are now talking with two other friends about the possibility of doing a volunteer project, probably for a local nursing home. This is very exciting to us. Anyway, thanks for sharing that and for providing the information needed on your Web page."*

Pat
Gate City, Virginia

### Note from Nancy

We were curious: How did Vallie possibly find the time, space and resources to produce so much for so many? One key, she said, was having a huge kitchen, where she cooks, sews and irons.

She keeps her ironing board set up all the time, and she constantly shares her table with craft projects. To speed construction, she keeps her sewing machine and serger side-by-side.

And, she laughs when she reminds us, "My house is topsy-turvy, often with the dishes undone and fabric all over the place." In other words, when you are just one person, creating at home and at this level of production, housekeeping can't be your top priority.

high-school home economics classes.

Vallie's been sewing ever since, often for philanthropy. Her project list could exhaust an 18-year-old.

She's made baby blankets to donate to a New Mexico mission, tablecloths for her church, head coverings for cancer patients undergoing chemotherapy, teaching dolls for troubled children, lap robes for nursing homes and sheets and bibs for a children's center.

### Too Busy for Awards

Recognition for her deeds is discouraged. Vallie is too busy starting new projects to take time for awards, no matter how well-deserved.

Resourcefulness and resilience are the keys to Vallie's volunteer efforts—and life. When given a carload of knit

*Tireless retiree Vallie Cole displays a quilt, one of many handcrafted items she makes for the needy.*

One Person *Can* Make a Difference

fabric, she made kids' T-shirts. When given some gabardine fabric, she created school jumpers.

Neither the death of her husband nearly 20 years ago nor the accidental disabling of her adult son, Wayne, has slowed her down. Vallie actually feels her own chronic ailment, fibromyalgia, a form of painful arthritis, keeps her focused on her task.

"I have to do something when I'm hurting or I can't sleep," Vallie relates. "I usually sew. It ends up giving me a few more productive hours, too."

Although most of us would struggle to match her production, we can borrow from Vallie's wise approach, revealed in her nomination for Washington Regional Medical Center's "Woman of the Year": "Serve and sew with a smile. This fine lady could be described in two words: caring and sharing."

Our guess is that Vallie Cole might not only be the most productive 72-year-old in Fayetteville, but possibly—in spirit—the richest as well.

# Giving the Lifelong Gift of a Skill
## Keith and Sharon Kerssen and the Colina de Luz Orphanage

MANY of us think of the Baja coast of Mexico, just south of San Diego, as a land of sun-warmed beaches and ocean breezes. But Keith and Sharon Kerssen know differently.

Each January for the past 10 years, they have traveled from their home in West St. Paul, Minnesota to work the winter months at the Colina de Luz orphanage, where they teach their students how to sew and to fix "just about everything," they say.

Because of the frequency and duration of their trips, the Kerssens know firsthand about the difficulties brought by the living conditions there.

### Winters Spell Hardships
"There is a lot of cold, damp weather in January, February, March and April," explains Sharon. "Evenings often get down to 45°F, and days do not get above 60°F. When it is raining, it is not very comfortable in a house that has no heat, possibly a dirt floor and window openings without glass."

That is why the ladies in Sharon's adult sewing class spend much of their time making curtains. Those coverings are not only needed for the windows, but also to divide the two or three small rooms in their homes, for the doorways

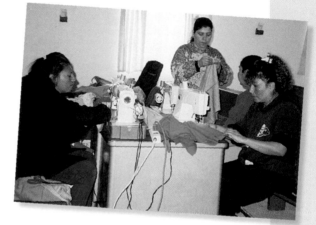

*Sharon Kerssen's Mexican friend Maria (standing) loves to help her teach students sewing skills.*

and for privacy in the outhouses.

In her children's sewing classes, Sharon starts with a simple pot holder, then moves on to easy sweatpants. "The kids also make zippered bags because we get many zippers donated," Sharon says.

In addition to zippers, the Kerssens rely on donations of fabric, sewing machine needles, thread (especially black and white), fabric scissors and elastic. Of course, the critical need is for sewing machines. Because Keith can "fix anything", he is able to keep machines

One Person *Can* Make a Difference

in good shape for Sharon's classes.

Residents of the orphanage are permitted to start learning to sew when they are 10 years old—and often can't wait to begin. Sharon laughs that when the Kerssens arrive each year, the kids run up to them yelling, "I'm 10! I'm 10!"

**Distance No Obstacle**

"The women who travel to our adult sewing classes are from the 18 poor churches the orphanage ministers to," Sharon relates.

"Sometimes classes are at a church. Often, though, they're held at the orphanage because the churches are very small. Some don't have electricity."

With donations of more sewing machines, the Kerssens could leave one or two at each church that has electricity for year-round sewing.

Why do Sharon and Keith visit Mexico during the coldest months? Winter is a good time to hold sewing classes because there are not many other activities available.

But more importantly, why do they go at all? Both Sharon and Keith love to volunteer, and working in Mexico is something they feel their faith has called them to do. They have no plans to stop anytime soon.

Despite having 12 grandchildren and family close by in Minnesota, Sharon feels they also have "real family down there" in Mexico. This devoted two-person team manages a sizable commitment to the Mexican "family" with joy, understanding and love.

**Teach a Man to Fish…**

Throughout this book, we have provided how-tos for projects that can

help others. The Kerssens offer another way of showing *Creative Kindness*—by teaching. The old adage applies here: "Give a man a fish and you feed him for a day; teach a man to fish and you feed him for a lifetime."

You don't have to travel thousands of miles. Why not reach out to scouting, 4-H, school and church groups in your own area? Teach people of all ages to sew, quilt, crochet, knit or repair sewing machines, and you give them a lifelong skill that they, in turn, can also share with others.

## Creative Kindness Goes to Cuba
### Jeannette Schilling—the Fig Leaf Ministry

SPEND just a few minutes with graphic designer Jeannette Schilling, and you are almost certain to fall under the spell of her colorful, animated and affectionate stories about her trips to Cuba.

Casting aside political agendas, economic embargoes, emigration controversies and ideological differences, Jeannette travels across North America from Oregon to teach her Cuban

One Person *Can* Make a Difference

friends how to sew undergarments.

But this *Creative Kindness* story did not begin with undergarments. First, Jeannette became involved with a non-denominational, nonprofit Christian organization that went to Cuba to provide Christian materials. At the same time, her team of four gave out basic items like medicine and toys.

"I was feeling like I wanted to do something to help others," Jeannette tells, "so I decided 'Why not?'"

After Jeannette's second trip, she was so in love with the people and the country that she wanted to extend her stay and offer additional help to Cubans. "The lightbulb just went on," Jeannette says.

"I may not be the greatest seamstress, but I knew there was a need for undergarments, and I also knew I could teach sewing. Undergarments seemed easy enough."

### Fig Leaf and Clothing Scarcity

She decided to call her group of one (so far) Fig Leaf Ministry. "It still makes me laugh," Jeannette says, "because I looked up 'sew' in the Bible, and the first reference was fig leaves — the first undergarments!"

And because they are such personal things, Jeannette felt it was a good way to get to know the women better.

In 2 weeks, Jeannette managed to get two sewing machines and initial supplies donated. She wasn't at all certain how she would organize her classes or get the word out, but she "just knew it would happen."

Indeed, it did. "We set up in the church, and somehow through the grapevine, word got out to the women," she recalls. What most amazed Jeannette, though, was that her first students—there were 14—told her that they had been praying for someone to teach them to sew undergarments.

Her students became "instant family", and though they had never seen a rotary cutter or a seam ripper, most knew how to sew and were eager to learn new techniques and try new patterns.

### Cuban Students: Able and Willing

The ladies could only stay a few

*Easy passage through Customs takes careful packing by Fig Leaf founder Jeannette Schilling.*

hours a day, 3 to 4 hours maximum, because of their families. During that time, Jeannette showed them how to make different kinds of undergarments, then left fabric and materials so the ladies could continue sewing.

For her next trip, Jeannette plans to set up a 6-day schedule of teaching and sewing. The students will work on three garments, and there will be patterns for children's sizes as well.

Although Jeannette has worked as part of a team, she has no qualms about making solo trips. "Cubans are warm, hospitable, social and giving, so it is easy to make friends," she notes. "They are also well-educated and like having someone to practice English with."

Jeannette hopes to go all over the island to teach. To raise money, she gives slide presentations in the United States. After one talk to a class of fifth and sixth graders, the kids collected both sewing notions and cash donations. Other tax-deductible gifts filter in through family and friends.

### No Boundaries to *Bondad Creativa*

Cuba is just 90 miles from Florida. The relatively small expanse of ocean between has seemed like a giant barrier, separating the countries for years.

Jeannette's work in Cuba is a wonderful example of our belief that there are no boundaries when it comes to *Creative Kindness*—also known to her Cuban friends as *Bondad Creativa*.

"When my children and I saw how we could help by donating fabric, I was reminded of some quilt squares that a friend had sent me. My children and I decided that we should send the squares to an organization featured on your show, so they could be helping someone out—instead of waiting for me! I am also going to go through my fabric scraps to see what else I can send. My children are going to help with this project, too. Your Web site makes it so simple to get in touch, and I'm sure it will bring out the best in people from all over the world. Thanks for sharing."

Michelle
Fayetteville, Georgia

One Person *Can* Make a Difference

The Project Linus Blanket and Quilting Bee was a HUGE success! Collectively, at every store, 112 quilted blankets were completed before the event closed at 5 p.m. There were many, many more quilts that volunteers took with them to finish later and return to the stores. And other volunteers took kits with them so they could create quilts at home. More than 400 people donated their time and loving labor to this project. We are very excited to talk with you about it.

Tammy
Seattle, Washington

# Caring with Quilts

## Think Globally, Create Locally

COUNTLESS CHILDREN— many of them seriously ill or emotionally or physically traumatized—are missing the security and therapy their own special blanket uniquely provides.

Several national and international organizations have been dedicated to producing and distributing this handmade comfort to children.

One Pacific Northwest fabric-store chain applied its own brand of retail ingenuity to a quilt-for-kids campaign—enlisting customers and store personnel—and in the process, multiplied blanket donations and the *Creative Kindness* spirit.

"For all of its uncertainty, we cannot flee the future...We must address and master the future together. It can be done if we restore the belief that we share a sense of national community, that we share a common endeavor. It can be done."

Congresswoman Barbara Jordan

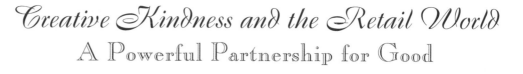

# Creative Kindness and the Retail World
## A Powerful Partnership for Good

CAN retail and charitable interests peacefully coexist? If the alliance that formed between Pacific Fabrics & Crafts and Project Linus is any example, not only can they coexist, together they can thrive.

Not long after the seven-store Northwest fabric chain joined forces with this charity, blanket and quilt donations to the Seattle area Project Linus chapters jumped from 75 to nearly 300 per month. Their mutually beneficial strategies could serve as blueprints for other retailers, large and small.

This partnership was the brainchild of former Pacific Fabric & Crafts ad-

*Volunteers and store personnel cut, sew and quilt at the Pacific Fabrics' multi-store "bee".*

vertising manager Tammy Carder who, during a leadership seminar, committed herself to community service.

As a retail executive, she knew how often charitable requests came in for supplies. But how could their stores really contribute, above and beyond sporadic donations and discounts?

Tammy knew a concerted program was needed, one that enlisted their willing and talented customers and staff and directed their efforts. Then, a light went on when a Project Linus volunteer called her about a discount. This senior had the time, but struggled to af-

ford the materials for the quilts.

**"Quilt Guilt" and Recruitment**

Tammy was convinced and soon convinced her Pacific associates that a union between their company and Project Linus could produce incredible results. With the help of her associates and the charity's area coordinators, Karen Knight and Lynn Mazer, she formulated a plan.

The first step was to answer the volunteers' two classic catch-22's: (1) "enough time, but not enough materials", and, conversely, (2) "too many materials, but not enough time" (also known as "quilt guilt").

To help solve these dilemmas and kick-start their Project Linus tie-in, the Pacific Fabrics & Crafts team came up with an ingenious fabric drive. Titled "Materialize This!", the program's collection concept was detailed in the advertising bulletin below:

*...Project Linus' Seattle chapter and Pacific Fabrics & Crafts are working in cooperation to collect fabrics for Project Linus volunteers. For each yard of fabric that you donate from your stash, Pacific Fabrics will reward your donation with 5% off a single-item purchase—up to 25%. If you've found quality fabrics in your stash that would be suitable for a washable, cuddly blanket of cotton, flannel or fleece and would like to make a donation to the Project Linus cause, drop off those yards at any Pacific Fabrics & Crafts location this month and receive your discount toward a future purchase.*

Hundreds of yards of fabric rolled into the seven stores. Generosity prevailed, and with it, garbage bags chock-full of donations.

With the discount they received,

some customers actually purchased more fabric to donate to the cause. Other customers came in with quilts ready-made for needy kids.

The second step was simple: Recruit customers and staff to make blankets and quilts utilizing the fabrics donated during the "Materialize This!" drive. The invitations and publicity went out in advertising circulars, store flyers and Project Linus publicity releases.

On one Sunday afternoon, the stores in the Seattle/Puget Sound region simultaneously hosted a "Blanket and Quilting Bee" with store-supplied cutting tools, notions, sewing machines and refreshments. Warm Products, Inc. donated the batting.

**No Contribution Too Small**

Volunteers were encouraged to join the quilt-making camaraderie, no matter what their skill or time limitations. Whenever possible to streamline quiltmaking, fabrics were precut into 4"-6" squares, readying them for assembly.

The event's welcoming flyer stated, "Everyone can contribute…we'll dedicate our efforts to giving every distressed child a security blanket made with love and care."

The bee was beyond Tammy's—and everyone's—expectations. "It was so inspiring," she says. "Even though people are incredibly busy, here they were, working side-by-side with people they didn't know—all for children. When they walked in the door, they were empowered to make a difference."

Participants numbered up to 50 per store, with each store producing as many as 100 quilts or kits for at-home completion. Though not limited to simple designs, basic quiltmaking was encouraged, such as the kind in Debbie Mumm's book, *Project Kids*. (Also see our design on page 48.)

Projects that weren't finished during the bee were taken home to be dropped off later. The Bremerton store customers alone finished 102 quilts, plus 90 more kits.

**Gifts of Warmth…and Love**

In keeping with tradition, donors personalized their creations with a spe-cial message for the recipient: "Made for You with Loving Care for Project Linus". It's easy to imagine children clinging to their custom-made quilt, much like this charity's cartoon namesake.

Pacific Fabrics committed to their philanthropic alliance and made the "Quilting for a Cause" fabric drive and quilting bee semi-annual events.

Volunteerism extended beyond the special events, too, as the stores became drop-off points for year-round donations. Project Linus then distributed the blankets to children in area hospitals, burn centers and shelters.

"For retailers, this alliance revealed the bright side of dealing with the public. It's refreshing to know our community in a different way," says Tammy. "It's so great to see customers as partners in a generous effort. I was overwhelmed with people's sacrifices—the victory of the human spirit."

**Note:** Since 1995, Project Linus chapters around the U.S. and the world have contributed more than 250,000 blankets to hospitals, crisis clinics, schools and social service agencies.

To find out if there is a Project Linus chapter in your area—or to learn about other similar groups, such as Binky Patrol—see "Connecting with Charities and Each Other" on page 94.

*Note from Nancy*

Karen Knight, Seattle area co-coordinator for Project Linus, reminds us that blankets can be knitted or crocheted as well as sewn.

She is an avid knitter herself, and she "always has a blanket in the works", which she carries with her everywhere.

A source for copyright-free instructions for one of Karen's favorite knitted blankets can be found on our Creative Kindness Reference List (see page 94).

*"When I first got into Project Linus, it was because I wanted to give back a little kindness that others—strangers—had offered me over the years. I also wanted to give children a sense of security that I didn't have growing up. I can provide this security through the blankets I make."*

Lynn
Federal Way,
Washington

# How You Can Quickly Assemble
## A Nine-Patch Quilt

*"During Christmas, Buster Bison of the Buffalo baseball team delivered quilts to all the children staying at Children's Hospital for the holidays. In one room was a lovely young teen with long hair. Her mom was in the bathroom, and when we entered the room, she was shocked to see Buster and shouted out. Her daughter started to laugh. The mom commented that this was the first time her daughter had laughed since being in the hospital. All the volunteers left the room crying tears of joy."*

Karen
Englewood,
Colorado

You might assume, as we did, that there was mainly one Project Linus quilt design used at the Pacific Fabrics & Crafts events. Not so. This charity wisely encouraged creative diversity, realizing the range of quilting expertise and available supplies.

Taking a cue from the Pacific Fabrics quilting sessions and our own teaching experiences, we designed a versatile nine-patch scheme.

Any beginner could tackle this simple patchwork, and any pro could easily embellish upon its basic design.

The nine-patch is amazingly adaptable to materials, too. As you can see from the chart on page 49, the range of patch/quilt sizes suits just about any fabric stash.

**If you make the quilt(s):** Divide and conquer—incorporate 1- to 2-hour sessions whenever possible throughout your schedule, and you'll have the nine-patch blocks and quilt completed before you know it. (The time required for each step varies, depending on the size of the quilt.)

**If your group makes the quilt(s):** Designate someone with quilting experience to serve as the quilt coordinator. Divide volunteers into several teams. Teams can specialize in a certain step

or steps—for instance, stitching the blocks—at each meeting.

Follow our five-step approach to streamline your "manufacturing". Obviously, step order must be maintained so that Step 2 follows Step 1, Step 3 follows Step 2 and so on.

## Supplies for One Nine-Patch Quilt

- **Assorted fabrics**—remnants or new yardage (see chart above right).

- **Backing (lining) fabric**—yardage or new or clean flat bed sheets.

- **Batting or new or clean blankets.**

- **Assorted sewing threads.**

- **Assorted yarns for tying quilts.**

- **Handy notions**—rotary cutter, mat and ruler; 1/4" (0.6 cm) quilting foot; seam gauge; safety pins or size 1 curved basting pins; Sewer's Fix-it Tape or masking tape (see page 94 for shopping information); chenille needle; iron; large table space.

# Nine-Patch Quilt: Five Simple Steps to Completion

## Step 1: Prepare quilt blocks.

- Cut 3-1/2" (9 cm) wide strips of two fabrics. Also cut plain 9-1/2" (24.3 cm) squares. The number of strips and blocks will depend on the size of the quilt (see chart below).

- Join strips to form two stratas, using accurate 1/4" (0.6 cm) seams. For Strata 1, join a Fabric A strip to each lengthwise edge of a Fabric B strip. Press seam allowances toward darker fabric.

  For Strata 2, join Fabric B strips to each lengthwise edge of a Fabric A strip. Press seam allowances toward darker fabric. Make as many stratas as needed for quilt's size.

- Cut stratas into 3-1/2" (9 cm) sections (see #1 below).

## Step 2: Stitch quilt blocks.

- Join sections to form the number of nine-patch blocks indicated in chart (see #2 below). For half the blocks, join two sections from Strata 1 to one section from Strata 2.

  For remaining blocks, join two sections from Strata 2 to one section from Strata 1. Position seam allowances in opposite directions on adjoining sections to reduce bulk.

*(Instructions continue on next page)*

| Quilt Size | 22" (56 cm) strips | | 45" (115 cm) strips | | # of 9-1/2" nine-patch blocks | # of plain 9-1/2" squares |
|---|---|---|---|---|---|---|
| | Fabric A | Fabric B | Fabric A | Fabric B | | |
| 36" x 36" (91.5 x 91.5 cm) | 6 | 6 | 3 | 3 | 8 | 8 |
| 36" x 45" (91.5 x 115 cm) | 9 | 9 | 6 | 6 | 10 | 10 |
| 45" x 63" (115 x 160 cm) | 15 | 15 | 9 | 9 | 18 | 17 |
| 54" x 81" (137 x 205.5 cm) | 21 | 21 | 12 | 12 | 27 | 27 |

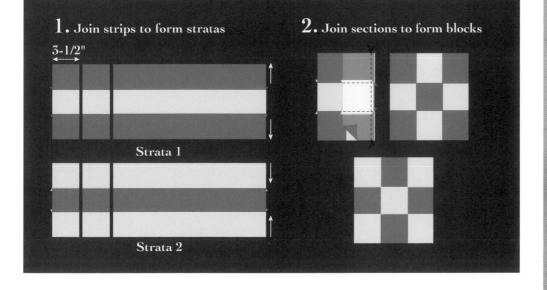

1. Join strips to form stratas

3-1/2"

Strata 1

Strata 2

2. Join sections to form blocks

### Step 3: Assemble quilt top.

- Lay out quilt, alternating pieced nine-patch blocks with 9-1/2" (24.3 cm) squares as shown below.

- Join blocks into rows. Then join rows to complete quilt top. Press seams flat, then to one side.

### Step 4: Layer and tie quilt.

- Cut backing at least 2" (3 cm) larger than quilt top on all sides.

- Tautly tape backing fabric to flat surface, wrong side up.

- Cut batting same size as backing. Center batting and quilt top (right side up) over backing.

- Pin layers together with safety pins or curved basting pins. Off-set pins so that the ties can be centered and added without unpinning.

- Use a sharp-point chenille needle and yarn or pearl cotton to tie and knot layers together in the center of each block.

### Step 5: Finish quilt.

- Trim batting even with the quilt top and edgestitch along all sides of quilt top, catching all layers.

- Trim backing so it extends 1" (2.5 cm) beyond quilt top on all sides.

- Meet cut edge of backing to cut edge of quilt top. Press.

- Fold backing over quilt top. Pin and edgestitch through all layers.

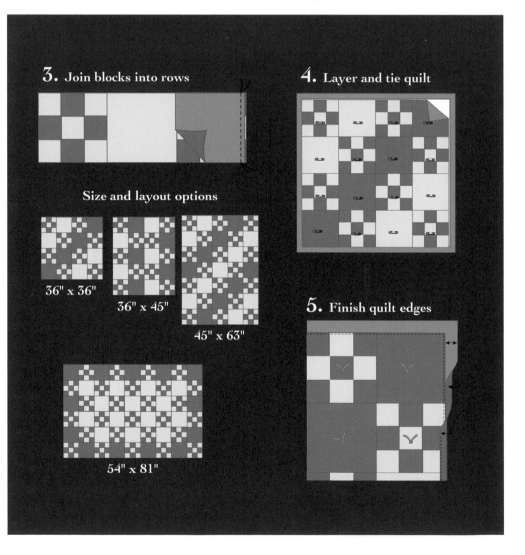

3. **Join blocks into rows**

**Size and layout options**

36" x 36"

36" x 45"

45" x 63"

54" x 81"

4. **Layer and tie quilt**

5. **Finish quilt edges**

Caring with Quilts

# Creative Kindness Continues
## Beautiful Warmth from "Ugly Quilts"

THE FIRST "Ugly Quilt" sleeping bags were developed by Flo Wheatley of My Brother's Keeper Quilt Group for the homeless in Pennsylvania. She dubbed the quilts "ugly" to "make sure volunteers weren't scared off by the quilting part" and in reference to the use of any available fabrics.

Her ingenious design created a quilt sack that a homeless person can crawl into for head-to-toe warmth. The Ugly Quilts can be tied with fabric straps or, for ready-made carrying handles, recycled men's ties.

Marlene Nelsen and her Iowa-based group of My Brother's Keeper quilters completed their 2,000th Ugly Quilt in the year 2000. On her Ugly Quilt instruction sheet, Marlene explains her volunteers' mission.

"We are individuals and groups who want to help the homeless," she details, "by making simple sleeping bags from clean, recycled fabrics and distributing them free of charge to people on the street who are cold."

Mitzi Luchtel, one of the quilters in the Iowa group, notes that many fab-

*Here's just a sampling of the "Ugly Quilts" My Brother's Keeper quilters made for the homeless.*

rics were donated after an article appeared in a local newspaper. Those "fabrics" included bedspreads, draperies and blankets from local resorts, as well as upholstery yardage from an area factory.

The following instructions are for our own adaptation of Flo's and Marlene's sleeping bag design ideas.

## How You Can Quickly Assemble
## An "Ugly Quilt" Sleeping Bag

**If you make the quilt(s):** Divide this multi-step project into 1- to 2-hour sessions, incorporating them whenever possible throughout your schedule. This way, you can finish a number of quilts in just a few weeks.

Each of the three steps will take about 60-90 minutes to complete, for a total of about 3 to 4-1/2 hours for each sleeping bag project.

**If your group makes the quilt(s):** Use our simple three-step approach on

page 52 to streamline your quilt "manufacturing". Divide participants into several teams. At each workstation, each team can specialize in a certain step or steps. Use large work surfaces to save time.

Teams can perform different steps at different meetings, or they can concentrate exclusively on one step. Obviously, step order must be managed so that Step 2 follows Step 1, Step 3 follows Step 2 and so on.

*(Instructions continue on next page)*

*"I am a pediatric nurse. In my spare time I would love to do some simple projects with small scraps. Once while visiting a child, I gave her a plain simple doll with no eyes. I saw this child 3 years later, and she was carrying the doll into surgery...it really does make a difference."*

Pat
(E-mail)

## Supplies for One Ugly Quilt

- **Large assortment of scrap fabrics, bedspreads or draperies.**
- **Batting, clean blankets or mattress pads.**
- **Neckties or fabric belts.**
- **Assorted sewing threads.**
- **Assorted crochet cotton or yarns.**
- **Handy notions**—rotary cutter, mat and ruler; size 1 curved basting pins; Sewer's Fix-it Tape or masking tape (see page 94 for shopping information); large-eyed hand embroidery needles; large table space.

# Ugly Quilt: Three Simple Steps to Completion

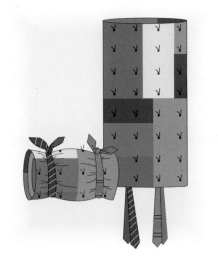

## Step 1: Create the sleeping bag cover.

- Cut an assortment of scrap fabrics, bedspreads or draperies into large squares or rectangles.
- Join fabric pieces, right sides together, to create two 7' (2.14 m) squares.
- Join the two squares, right sides together, to complete the 7' x 14' (2.14 m x 4.27 m) sleeping bag cover. Zigzag or serge outer edges to prevent raveling.
- Add two pairs of 3' (91.5 cm) straps,

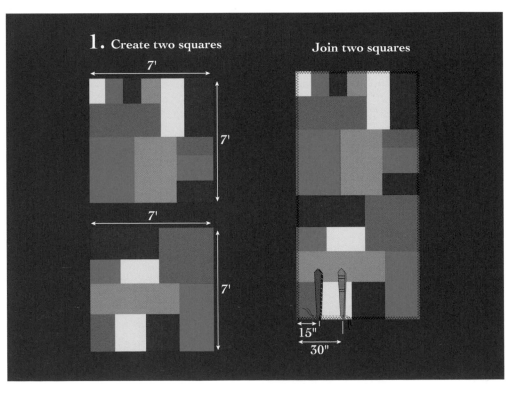

1. **Create two squares**

7'

7'

7'

7'

**Join two squares**

15"

30"

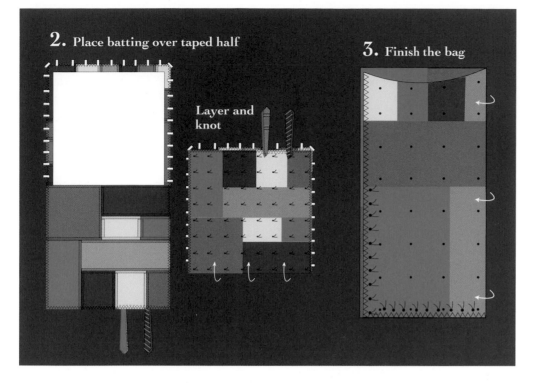

**2.** Place batting over taped half

Layer and knot

**3.** Finish the bag

using neckties or fabric belts. Stitch the pairs of ties or belts along one 7' (2.14 m) edge, approximately 15" (38 cm) and 30" (76 cm) from corner.

## Step 2: Layer and knot the quilt.

- The following steps will be easier if three 8' x 4' (2.44 m x 1.22 m) tables are positoned to create an 8' x 12' (2.44 m x 3.66 m) work surface.

- Lay sleeping bag cover, face down, on table surface. Using Sewer's Fix-it Tape or masking tape, secure one 7' (2.14 m) half to table to prevent cover from shifting.

- Place batting material over taped half, leaving a 3" (7.5 cm) seam allowance on the three raw edges.

- Fold untaped half of cover over batting. Pin along edges if necessary.

- Tie and knot through all layers using yarn or a double strand of crochet cotton, spacing knots 8" (20.5 cm) apart.

- Fold straps toward center of tied quilt, away from edges. Remove tape from quilt.

## Step 3: Fold and tie quilt into sleeping bag.

- Fold tied quilt in half, meeting opposite cut edges to form a 3-1/2' x 7' (1.07 m x 2.14 m) sleeping bag.

- Triple knot bottom edge and about halfway up the open side of the bag using yarn or a double strand of crochet cotton. Space knots 3" (7.5 cm) apart, catching only the four cover layers but not the batting.

    We recommend hand-stitching the layers together instead of machine-stitching because of the bulk created by the fabric and batting.

- Turn sleeping bag right side out. Roll bag; tie straps tightly.

*Note from Nancy*

Make a child-size sleeping bag in the same way, using two 5' (1.53 m) squares and substituting ribbon or trims for the neckties.

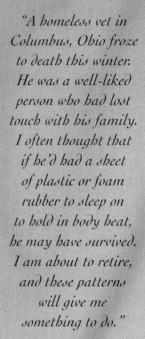

*"A homeless vet in Columbus, Ohio froze to death this winter. He was a well-liked person who had lost touch with his family. I often thought that if he'd had a sheet of plastic or foam rubber to sleep on to hold in body heat, he may have survived. I am about to retire, and these patterns will give me something to do."*

L.Z.
Columbus, Ohio

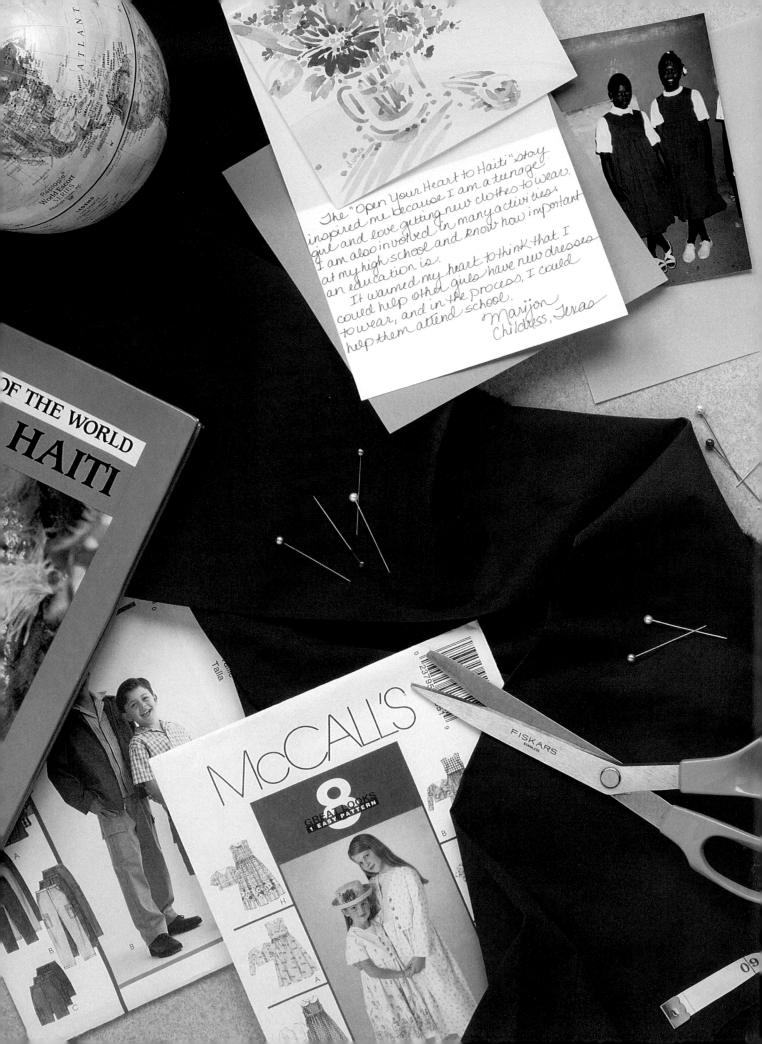

The "Open Your Heart to Haiti" story inspired me because I am a teenage girl and love getting new clothes to wear. I am also involved in many activities at my high school and know how important an education is.

It warmed my heart to think that I could help other girls have new dresses to wear, and in the process, I could help them attend school.

Marijon
Childress, Texas

To: RSVP Center
c/o Open Your Heart to Haiti
1835 North Stevens Street
Rhinelander, WI    Zip: 54501

CREATIVE
KINDNESS

# Open Your Heart to The World...

## And Renew Your Faith in Humanity

SEEING just one person actually make a difference in the world renews our confidence in our ability to do the same.

Real people, like Jackie Bushong-Martin, Arlene Miller, Marijon Benham and their fellow "Open Your Heart to Haiti" volunteers, are cultivating *Creative Kindness* to serve humanity.

Somehow, these people are finding the time and mustering resources to create uniforms that change lives. Seeing the vitality of their service and spirit gives us, their Haitian friends and our needy world hope.

"OUR OWN SUCCESS, TO BE REAL, MUST CONTRIBUTE TO THE SUCCESS OF OTHERS."
ELEANOR ROOSEVELT

# Open Your Heart to Haiti
## Making Uniforms—and Changing Lives

LIFE'S NECESSITIES—food, fresh water, clothing, medical supplies—commonplace only a few hundred miles away in America, are scarce in many regions of Haiti.

As part of a medical-missionary team sent to that Caribbean island country in 1995, Jackie Bushong-Martin witnessed the daily suffering caused

*Jackie Bushong-Martin, Open Your Heart to Haiti founder, poses with Haitian children wearing their new school uniforms for the first time.*

by these conditions, particularly among the youth.

Yet, while living with Haitian families, Jackie was moved by the children's resilience—their eagerness to learn, their happy greetings in English, their beautiful singing and, despite the hot sun and deplorable conditions, their hopeful forbearance.

In a place where malnutrition is an everyday occurrence and homes may only be small, dirt-floored tin lean-tos, schooling for children can be limited—or non-existent. Literacy rates remain at some of the lowest in the world, and girls are underrepresented in Haiti's tiny school populations.

It wasn't until her first mission trip to this country that Jackie learned why.

**Uniforms = Schooling = Survival**

"I discovered that the government requires all children to wear a uniform to attend school," she recounts. "It sounds so simple to us, just a dress of a certain color and shoes for the girls.

"But when there's barely enough money for food, a school uniform is a luxury beyond the reach of most Haitian families. There are thousands of children who cannot meet these requirements and, without help, will never be able to go to school."

In her travels throughout villages there, Jackie also observed that uniforms meant much more than schooling. Only those Haitian children who attend school are eligible for the modest daily meal of rice, beans or millet.

So, yes, a uniform meant school. But it also meant a higher likelihood of survival—and, just possibly, a future.

**Can-Do Seniors Join In**

When Jackie explained to her sister, Lori Stroede, about the lack of uniforms—and thus, education and meals—the two arrived at an action plan:

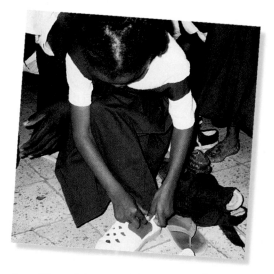

*Open Your Heart to Haiti program volunteers provide Haitian children with new shoes as well as handmade uniforms so they may attend school.*

Open Your Heart to the World…

Enlist the organizational and sewing talents of the Retired and Senior Volunteer Program (RSVP), a group Lori directs in Rhinelander, Wisconsin.

These capable seniors readily accepted the challenge of producing the basic uniforms, acquiring the companion shoes and blouses and helping coordinate shipments to Haiti. Jackie christened their campaign "Open Your Heart to Haiti".

She and Lori set an ambitious, long-term goal of providing 2,400 sets of uniforms and other clothing needed by children in Haiti's Port-de-Paix region. Both women continue to be inspired by the enthusiastic, can-do attitude of their senior recruits, despite the rigors of this production level.

"Our gift is in the giving," Jackie tells. "Our volunteers, especially the homebound, are able to do something constructive with their free time.

"They are also able to directly impact a program, rather than just send money. Many of our men volunteers toured war-torn countries during their service in World War II, so they can relate to the plight of Haiti and the children there."

### Nationwide Awareness

News about Open Your Heart to Haiti spread to WJFW, the local NBC affiliate, which aired a report about their uniform-making efforts. Viewer Ruth Ann Richardson then contacted Jackie, volunteering to sew uniforms, and also wrote to Nancy's Notions asking for material donations.

Because of Ruth Ann's referral, we interviewed Jackie and Lori—and Open Your Heart to Haiti was chosen to be featured on the "Sew a Smile" segment of *Sewing with Nancy*.

Being showcased on my PBS show and Nancy's Notions' companion Web site catapulted Open Your Heart to Haiti into nationwide awareness. Volunteers and contributions multiplied dramatically.

Jackie now estimates that over 75% of their cash, material and sewing donations are a direct result of their story being told on *Sewing with Nancy*. The overwhelming response was unexpected—and gratifying.

"When this program started, it was just me, trying to make a difference in a few needy children's lives. I never imagined it would grow like this," admits Jackie.

Like the RSVP volunteers, *Sewing with Nancy* viewers throughout the United States and Canada welcomed the opportunity to help Haitian children. Their letters are testimony to

*Dedicated Retired and Senior Volunteer Program (RSVP) volunteers from St. Croix, Wisconsin proudly show their handmade Open Your Heart to Haiti uniforms and participation certificates.*

the contagious kindness spread by willing hands and open hearts.

Every letter fuels Lori's passion for Open Your Heart to Haiti and her confidence in mankind.

### Discovering Goodness

"There are a lot of people left in this world who truly care about others—we aren't so bad after all!" Lori says. "I am especially hopeful when I receive letters such as the one from high school student Marijon Benham (see page 66). Some of our youth do care.

"To be honest, the most satisfying part of my work with the Haitian people is the response of those who have come forward to help," Lori adds. "It seems that all we hear these days is negative news about how our society is going downhill.

"I was amazed by how many peo-

*"I saw your program showing clothing to sew for children in Haiti. This was really an eye-opener for me because I am retired and would love to do this. Maybe we can organize church groups. We have time to get started and would love helping those precious children."*

Sara
(E-mail)

Open Your Heart to the World…

ple have reached out to our program. It restores my faith in people! I read letters (such as the one shared below left) and I just cry."

To date, Open Your Heart to Haiti has sent or delivered nearly 700 uniforms, complete with shoes, socks and blouses. True to her person-to-person philosophy, Jackie made a third trip to Haiti April 10-22, 2000, during which she delivered several hundred more school ensembles.

Her spring itinerary also included Cap-Haitien, a northern Haitian town of 250,000, where she assessed the need for uniforms—and is now determined to extend her ministry.

Thanks to Jackie's seemingly inexhaustible energy and vision and the help of hundreds of Open Your Heart to Haiti volunteers, Haitian children are discovering reading, writing, arithmetic, the nourishment of a daily meal —and that someone in North America cares about them.

American and Canadian volunteers, in turn, are discovering their own, and each others', goodness.

# How You Can
## Open Your Heart to Haiti

When you face a situation that seems overwhelming, Jackie Bushong-Martin is the kind of person you want to have in your address book. She knew that tackling poverty was far beyond her abilities. But if Haiti's children could receive an education, they would be the country's hope for the future.

And, if uniforms were the only obstacle, then she would make uniforms! She used her talents as an organizer to round up a group of enthusiastic volunteers and to solicit supplies. Calling on the Retired and Senior Volunteer Program was an inspired solution.

Open Your Heart to Haiti uniforms are exactly that—uniform. They must, by Haitian regulation, be made to exacting color and design requirements (see the "Note from Nancy" at right).

In this section, you will learn how many different solutions you can find to meet a single need like school uniforms. Once you start looking around your own community, you're bound to come up with even more.

### Finding Volunteers and Getting Organized

• The Retired and Senior Volunteer Program (RSVP) is a national organization with local offices in all 50 states, the District of Columbia, Puerto Rico and the Virgin Islands. It is part of the National Senior Service Corps program, which is part of the Corporation for National Service.

RSVP helps people age 55 and older put their skills and life experience to work in their communities. Nearly half

## Note from Nancy

In an effort to provide the most accurate pattern, fabric, supply and contact information, we recommend that you visit our Web site (www.creativekindness.com) or write to us (see page 94).

On our Creative Kindness Reference List, which is updated regularly, you'll find important particulars for Open Your Heart to Haiti uniform-making—required patterns and fabrics, plus sources.

Also featured is an extensive list of all the charities that we've profiled in this book. They include the Open Your Heart to Haiti RSVP Center and the national RSVP office.

a million RSVP volunteers currently work from a few hours each week to the equivalent of full-time jobs.

Contact an RSVP office to present the idea of making school uniforms (see the "Note from Nancy" on page 58).

● Consider Open Your Heart to Haiti as a project for junior high, high school and youth classes or groups. The simple uniforms teach basic sewing and organizational skills: fabric preparation, efficient assembly order, pattern cutting, seams, facings, zippers and finishing.

For a comprehensive class lesson plan, students could also report on the food, customs, geography and art of Haiti. This island country has a rich and colorful history.

● Don't overlook the homebound and disabled. There are many people with sewing or other skills just waiting for an invitation to help. They may be limited in mobility, but not in spirit.

Place public service announcements

*Young Haitians look forward to receiving school uniforms and to the benefits education will bring.*

in your local newspaper and on radio and television explaining that anyone who sews can make Open Your Heart to Haiti uniforms at home. Recruit other volunteers to drop off supplies and pick up the finished uniforms.

# How You Can Quickly Assemble
# Uniforms for Haitian Girls and Boys

**If you make the uniform(s):** Divide and conquer—incorporate 1- to 2-hour sessions throughout your schedule, and you'll have a jumper, shirt or pants finished in only a few days. (Each of the five steps for each garment will take about 2 hours, for a total of about 10 hours for each entire project.)

**If your group makes the uniform(s):** Use our five-step approach for each project to streamline your "manufacturing": At each work session, complete the same step on several garments. Our recommendation is that each team specialize in a certain step or steps.

Teams can perform different steps at each meeting, or they can all concentrate on one step. Obviously, step order must be managed so that Step 2 follows Step 1, Step 3 follows Step 2 and so on.

## Supplies for Uniforms

The Haitian government will only accept uniforms made to their fabric and design specifications. To the best of our ability, we've provided accurate general requirements in the following list.

However, because we don't know when you'll be reading this material, we've listed the specific patterns and fabrics you'll need on our continually updated Reference List available on our Web site or by mail. Please check the list before proceeding with these projects (see page 94).

### Girl's Jumper
● Pattern for the jumper must include the design details shown on page 60: jewel neckline, sleeveless, zipped back seam with high waistline and gathered skirt. Sizes can range from
*(List continues on next page)*

Toddler 2 to Misses 12 (the smallest and largest sizes are needed most).

- Fabric must be broadcloth color #83682 (burgundy/claret) under the brand name of either Palencia or TrÈ Mode.

- Pockets are optional, but lace, trim and appliques are not permitted.

### Boy's Shirt and Pants
- Patterns for the boy's uniform must include the details shown at right: shirt—notched collar, short sleeves, single-button front and left breast pocket; pants—slightly gathered into banded waistband and fly-zippered front. Sizes can range from Toddler 3 to Boys 14.

- Fabric must be white broadcloth for the shirt and broadcloth color #83682 (burgundy/claret) for the pants.

### Preparations
- Consult your pattern guidesheets for specific instructions. Then adapt the construction of the garments into the simple-to-sew steps that follow.

- Preshrink by pre-washing and line-drying the fabric.

## Girl's Jumper: Five Simple Steps to Completion

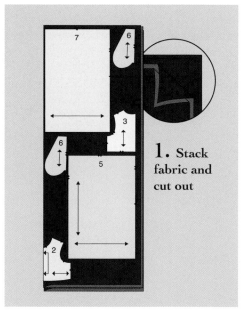

**1. Stack fabric and cut out**

### Step 1: Cut out and finish the edges.
- Cut out two or more jumpers at the same time. Stack two folded layers

of fabric and pin the pattern pieces through all layers. You'll be amazed at how fast and easy cutting can be!

- Zigzag or serge to finish all cut edges.

Open Your Heart to the World…

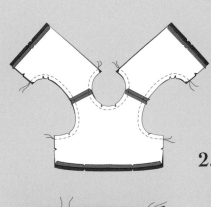

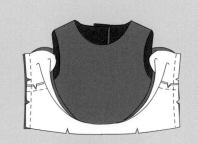

**2.** Create the bodice

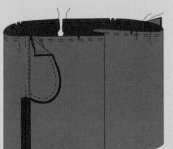

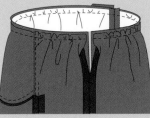

**3.** Attach the skirt

**4.** Insert a centered zipper

**5.** Finish the jumper

## Step 2: Create the bodice.

- Stitch the shoulder seams of both the bodice and the lining.
- Stitch the bodice and lining together at the neckline and armholes.
- Stitch the side seams.

## Step 3: Attach the skirt.

- Stitch the pockets to the skirt.
- Stitch the side seams.
- Gather the waistline.
- Stitch the skirt to the bodice.

## Step 4: Insert centered zipper.

- Insert the zipper in the center back seam.
- Tack the lining at the center back and waistline.

## Step 5: Finish the jumper.

- Hand-stitch a hook and eye to the top of the zipper.
- Hem the skirt.

Open Your Heart to the World...

# Boy's Shirt: Five Simple Steps to Completion

## Step 1: Cut—fuse—zigzag.

- Cut out two or more shirts at the same time. Stack two folded layers of fabric and pin the pattern pieces through all layers. For ease of cutting, use an electric scissors or a rotary cutter and cutting mat.

### Note from Nancy

White broadcloth is the fabric selected by the Haitian government for the boy's shirt. Unlike the jumper and pants, there is not a specific color number of fabric to purchase. Remember to refer to page 60 for the required design details.

### Note from Nancy

The pattern guidesheet may not suggest this sewing sequence, but the pocket and collar can easily be sewn in a 2-hour setting. Both elements are small and easy to handle. I like to sew them at the same time.

- Zigzag or serge all the cut edges.

- Using fusible interfacing, fuse interfacing to the wrong side of the shirt facing and collar. (If the pattern calls for sew-in interfacing, streamline the process by using fusible interfacing. It's very durable and extremely easy and fast to use.)

## Step 2: Create a pocket and collar.

- Stitch the pocket to the left shirt front.

- Stitch the collar so that it is ready to attach to the neckline.

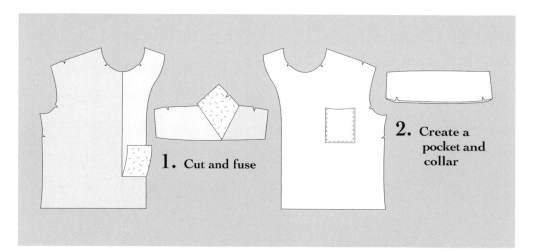

1. Cut and fuse

2. Create a pocket and collar

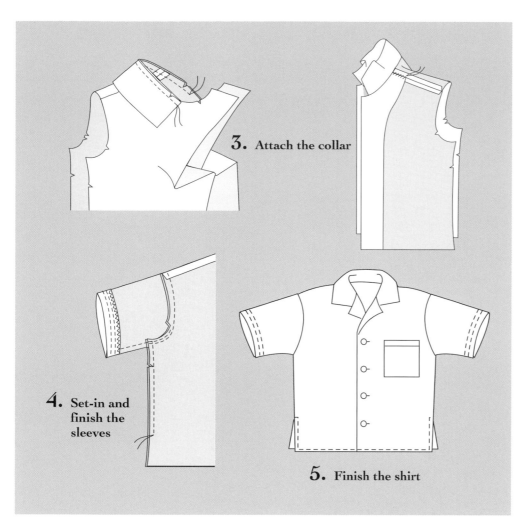

**3.** Attach the collar

**4.** Set-in and finish the sleeves

**5.** Finish the shirt

## Step 3: Attach the collar.

- Stitch the shoulder seams.
- Machine-baste the collar to the neck edge.
- Finish the neckline by stitching the facing in place.

## Step 4: Set-in and finish the sleeves.

- Stitch the sleeves to the armholes.
- Stitch the underarm seams.
- Machine-stitch the sleeve hems.

## Step 5: Finish the shirt.

- Machine-stitch the shirt hems.
- Machine-stitch buttonholes. Hand-stitch the buttons in place.

*Note from Nancy*

Will you be working with several other volunteers? If so, I recommend creating specialized workstations for each step of the construction process (also see my "Note from Nancy" on page 65).

For instance, find out which participants enjoy stitching buttonholes. Then assign those people to be the experts at your "buttonhole station".

Put your best buttonhole-making machine (or machines) at this station. (Some machines are better for buttonholes than others.)

Open Your Heart to the World…

# Boy's Pants: Five Simple Steps to Completion

## Step 1: Cut—fuse—zigzag.

- Cut out two or more pants at the same time. Stack two folded layers of fabric and pin the pattern pieces through all layers. For ease of cutting, use an electric scissors or a rotary cutter and cutting mat to cut through the layers.

- Zigzag or serge to finish all the cut edges.

- Using fusible interfacing, fuse interfacing to the waistband pieces.

## Note from Nancy

Like the girl's jumper, the boy's pants must be made out of a specific burgundy broadcloth and must include specific design details (see page 60).

Some pants patterns feature both side and cargo pockets. On the boy's uniform, the cargo pockets are optional.

For speed and ease, just the side pockets are used in our instructions. Check the pattern guidesheet if you'd also like to incorporate cargo pockets into the construction order.

Don't be discouraged—all sewing involves simple techniques. Just follow the easy steps here.

## Step 2: Stitch front details.

- Insert the front zipper.

- Stitch the pocket facing and pocket inset to the pant front.

- Stitch the waistband pieces to the pant front, matching the notches.

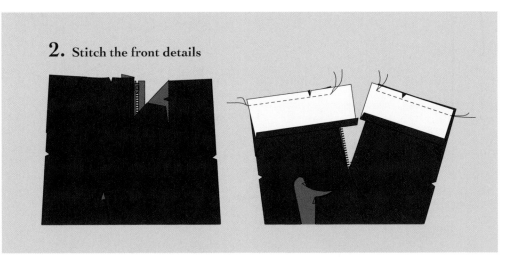

**2.** Stitch the front details

Open Your Heart to the World…

# Step 3: Stitch back details.

- Stitch the center back seam.

- Press under a casing; stitch. Insert the elastic.

# Step 4: Stitch long seams.

- Stitch the front to the back at the side seams.

- Stitch the inside leg seams.

- Place one leg inside the other; stitch the remaining crotch seam.

# Step 5: Finish the waistband and hem.

- Stitch the front edges of the waistband together.

- Fold the inside of the waistband to cover the waistline seam. Machine- or hand-stitch.

- Hand-stitch a hook and eye to the waistband.

- Hem the pants, using a machine straight stitch.

*Note from Nancy*

This school uniform project is ideal for assembly-line construction.

Set up six to eight long tables. Assign fabric preparation and cutting—great jobs for non-sewers—to the first one or two tables. Put sewing machines on the next three to four tables, with ironing boards and irons in between.

Once patterns have been cut out, your multi-talented cutters will become pressers. Table three is for inserting zippers.

Then move on to table four for sewing facings, while table five provides the finishing touches. The last table is in charge of final inspection and folds the uniforms for packing and shipping.

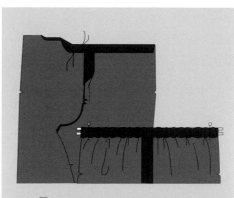

**3.** Stitch the back details

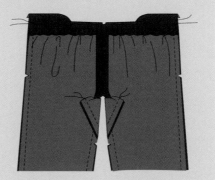

**4.** Stitch the long seams

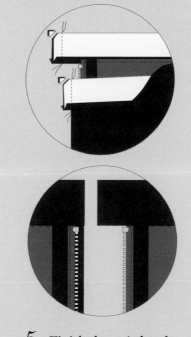

**5.** Finish the waistband (no hem shown)

*"I have a group of special education high school students. They have always received donated gifts through various organizations, and I am looking for a project that they can do this year to be of service to someone else. Open Your Heart to Haiti would be perfect."*

Ann
(E-mail)

# Reactions to Open Your Heart to Haiti—and Actions

ONCE you talk with Arlene Miller of Crofton, Kentucky, assures Jackie Bushong-Martin, you'll know what "team player" truly means. Arlene's motto is "I will do whatever I am meant to do." That's why she has made over four trips to Haiti to bring clothing, education and Bible study.

But, Arlene admits, taking that first step was not easy. "I was seeing all these things about Haiti," she explains. "I felt God wanted me to go, but I kept arguing. We have needy people right here at home."

One day, she watched *Sewing with Nancy* and, as luck would have it, the program featured Open Your Heart to Haiti. Arlene quit her mental debates, contacted Jackie and, in March 1998, this 58-year-old made her first trip to the island with a Crusades for Christ team and 70 uniforms.

Her health care background helped Arlene deal both emotionally and physically with the Haitians she met. They included a range of ages, from children to adults. "Little miracles"

*In Haiti, where even basic necessities are scarce, challenges can seem insurmountable. But as volunteer Arlene Miller discovered, each small act of kindness and generosity makes a big difference.*

*From Arlene Miller's bright smile, it is difficult to imagine that on her first trip to Haiti, she often cried about the huge challenge she had undertaken.*

were realized, too—one group of Haitian men worked to repair an unsafe bridge between two villages that once had traded hostilities.

"Every day was an experience," she recalls. "I couldn't really see God at work, but then I realized God is using us to chip away at problems."

Although she never intended to go back, Arlene always seems to be planning the next trip, packing uniforms and an endlessly giving spirit.

"Once I had 53 T-shirts with me, and wouldn't you know?" she smiles. "We found an orphanage with 53 kids."

# Yes, Young People Can—and Do— Make a Difference

THOUGH just a high school junior, Marijon Benham believes that she can make a difference in peoples' lives. During an interview, Marijon discussed her many charitable projects

and her guiding belief: "To the world you may just be someone, but to someone, you may be the world."

The Open Your Heart to Haiti story inspired this Childress, Texas teen-

Open Your Heart to the World...

ager in particular because it involved sewing for that "someone"—another girl. "And I know how special you feel when you have something new to wear," she adds.

Marijon spends her own money to buy the Haitian uniform supplies. She recorded this international community service for her 4-H club work.

The avid seamstress has been cultivating her hobby since third grade, and hopes to recruit other teens to sew and utilize their skills for charity. Her best friend now helps make Open Your

*Childress, Texas high school volunteer Marijon Benham donates sewing supplies and expertise to assemble uniforms for the Open Your Heart to Haiti program.*

Heart to Haiti uniforms.

Marijon's career goal is to be a pediatric nurse. The possibility seems strong that one day she might travel to Haiti herself, delivering uniforms, medical know-how and her special *Creative Kindness*.

*Lori Stroede (far right) demonstrates pattern cutting techniques to Haitian women during a sewing class. Students use treadle machines whenever electricity is unavailable.*

### Note from Nancy

In addition to providing uniforms, Lori Stroede, Jackie Bushong-Martin's sister, was determined to bring sewing skills to Haiti.

Not only could her students share this newfound talent with their families, but they could enhance their educational and occupational opportunities as well.

**Atlantic Ocean**

Port-de-Paix

Cap-Haitien

**Caribbean Sea**

N W E S

**HAITI**

Jérémie

★ Port-au-Prince

Les Cayes

"As part of my 4-H clothing project, I am enclosing two uniforms. My prayer is that whoever gets to wear them will do so in good health. It made my heart happy to be able to do something for someone else. The 'Sewing with Nancy' Internet connection has given me many opportunities to do more community service. Thanks for having your information on this site. I am a junior in high school and love 4-H."

Marijon
Childress, Texas

Open Your Heart to the World...

I'd like a list of organizations that accept donations of fabric. My daughter and I saw the "Sew a Smile" series on T.V. It gave us an idea of what we could do with our unwanted sewing supplies. We want to send them to someone who can use them.

Paula
Ames, Iowa

# Creative Kindness Knows No Walls

## Redefining Our Community

AS you probably know, prisons are a growth industry in America. What you may not know is that inside these institutions are sincere and dedicated workers for charity projects.

We found that in helping others, inmates help rehabilitate themselves. The joy and therapy of giving cannot be shut out by prison walls.

And when *Creative Kindness* is cultivated among this seemingly unlikely community, they become part of our community, both in effort and in spirit.

"Love yourself first and everything else falls into line. You really have to love yourself to get anything done in this world."

Lucille Ball

# Community Service at the Wisconsin Correctional Institution for Women
## Building Skills, Productivity and Self-Esteem

YOU can call her "Shania", she says. She is fresh-faced, with blonde hair pulled back in a ponytail. Shania volunteered for this program because there were no other jobs available, and she liked the idea of "doing stuff for the community".

So far, this "stuff" includes 150 crocheted hat, mitten and scarf sets for needy kids at a local YMCA. Shania, 23, is an inmate at the Wisconsin Correctional Institution (WCI) in Taycheedah, and she works in the prison's community service program. Her prison roommate taught her to crochet.

The small village of Taycheedah (rhymes with "Velveeta") is snuggled between the waters of Lake Winnebago and the wooded hills of central Wiscon-

*Multicolored "quillows" made by inmates at the Wisconsin Correctional Institution in Taycheedah are ready for donation to area charities.*

sin. If you can ignore the wire-topped fence and the armed guards, entering WCI feels like walking onto a college campus. A brick building with columns looks out on a well-kept lawn. Small groups of women sit at picnic tables.

Within the walls of Wisconsin's largest maximum-security facility for women, inmates work, go to class and visit with each other.

There is at Taycheedah an energy and sense of purpose—everyone seems productively busy. Walking through the modern education building with Assistant Warden Mark Heise, you can forget you are in a prison. But of course, when your visit is over, you can leave.

### Faith in Human Goodness

As Warden Heise talks about the accomplishments of Taycheedah's community service program, his commitment and pride are obvious.

A woman from nearby Fond du Lac started the program in 1994. This dedicated volunteer saw the inmates of Taycheedah as a great untapped resource for community good.

Why not, she reasoned, show these women how to help the community, build their self-confidence and teach them a marketable skill? But it took courage, patience and a fundamental belief in people to convince the administration of a prison—and inmates—that this program would work.

Today, prison shelves are stacked with stitchery, from cozy "quillows" destined for a Salvation Army facility to stacks of brightly colored mittens, hats and scarves ready for the YMCA and stunning handmade afghans bound for nursing homes.

Hundreds of people, including the inmates, are benefiting from one woman's faith in the human heart and her willingness to look for kindness in a creative way. By extending a hand to women overlooked by much of society, she found that kindness can bloom in unexpected places.

### Creative Rehabilitation

Initially, the Taycheedah program focused on teaching inmates sewing skills and on producing quillows (for

Creative Kindness Knows No Walls

a description and directions, see page 72) for area shelters and foster homes.

As originally established, all work continues to be distributed anonymously—recipients are not aware of the origin of donated items. Church and other charity groups provide the fabric and other materials needed.

In 1997, the prison assumed direct management of the program. While inmates still make quillows when donations permit, the cost of supplies makes continuous production impossible.

Because yarn, knitting needles and crochet hooks are easier to come by, the inmates now knit and crochet hats, caps, scarves, mittens, afghans, baby buntings, infant clothing and other hand-stitched items.

The program is also organized and run like a small business. A community organization contracts for a specific number of items by a certain date. The contracting organization also agrees to provide the supplies. Once they have a contract, the inmates go to work.

Full-time participants in the program work from 8 to 11 a.m. and 1 to 4 p.m., Monday through Friday. They are currently paid 23¢ per hour by the state of Wisconsin, with wages designated for the inmate's release.

### Style a High Priority

Careful attention is given to aesthetics. Girls' mittens are made in pastels with flowers and hearts in the design. Boys' get bold greens and blues or sports team colors.

Inmates are creative and opinionated. "I have to match the colors," Shania says excitedly. "*No* clashing colors. It has to be cute."

Shania is forthright about her involvement. "Instead of doing something stupid, I help somebody else," she says. "I feel good about myself when I help somebody."

One officer guards the room and may occasionally be called on for advice, but teaching is largely done by peers. Inmates often make up their own patterns and pass them on to others. There is, of course, friendly competition and showing off of items that rival any-

*The Taycheedah community service workroom is busy with quillow cutting and sewing activities.*

thing you find in the best stores.

### Learning and Self-Discovery

Rehabilitation is a benefit of this program as well. "Mary", 42, has big brown eyes and rings of curls around her pretty face. A recovering addict, she views her service as essential to recovery.

Mary came to the program already knowing how to crochet. Like Shania, Mary is very concerned about how her work looks, adding special accents like crocheted roses to girls' hats.

"Don't throw things together. Coordinate because you care," she advises.

For Mary, service is part of rehabilitation and restitution. She is learning to be responsible, to conduct herself appropriately and to discover her abilities. "You can make this experience be what you want. You can leave prison in your mind and work on how your life will be when you get out."

### *Creative Kindness* Redefined

Gail and I included this section on Taycheedah's community service program not to trivialize or glamorize prison life or the actions that sent these people to prison. Our objective was to show how, when you search for kindness, your reach can extend to the participants as well as to the projects.

Seeing Taycheedah's success opened our eyes to, and changed our perception of, *Creative Kindness*.

*"This program boosts my self-esteem, teaches me to be patient and helps me relax. It is important to be able to complete something—to begin and finish. I was so proud of my first hat that I stayed with it."*

"Mary"
Taycheedah,
Wisconsin

Creative Kindness Knows No Walls

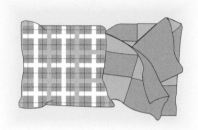

Folded in its own case, a quillow is a pillow. Unfolded, a quillow is a quilt. Although these practical, comfy quilt/pillow combos can be created in many ways, we recommend the following two methods. Choose the one that best utilizes your supplies, sewing time and expertise.

The first, the **Patchwork Quillow**, is made from readily available, woven cotton fabrics. Because this patchwork quillow combines odds and ends of fabrics, it is the perfect project for programs such as the one at the Wisconsin Correctional Institution, which relies on donated supplies.

Our second, the **Fleece Quillow**, is made from popular hi-loft fabrics such as Polarfleece® or Eskimo Fleece. It is the quickest to make of all the quillows, requiring a minimum of cutting and sewing time.

The fleece fabric's unique characteristics—reversible, lightweight, warm, lush nap, ravel-free—eliminate the need for batting, seam or edge finishing and multiple layers. Only three rows of stitching are required!

However, fleeces are seldom donated to charitable sewing or quilting groups. Plan on purchasing the fabric required (see "Supplies for One Fleece Quillow" on page 73).

But there's good news—the speed, sewing ease and "forgiving" loft of this low-maintenance material balances the costs incurred.

**If you make the patchwork quillow(s):** Divide and conquer—incorporate 1- to 2-hour sessions when possible throughout your schedule, and you'll have the patch blocks and quillow completed in a few days.

**If your group makes the patchwork quillow(s):** Divide participants into teams. Each team can specialize in a certain step or steps at each meeting.

Follow our five-step approach to streamline your "manufacturing". Obviously, step order must be maintained so that Step 2 follows Step 1, Step 3 follows Step 2 and so on.

**If you or your group make the fleece quillow(s):** Quick cutting and super-simple two-step construction means little, if any, need for "dividing and conquering". If you make the quillow by yourself, cutting and sewing can be completed in just a 1-hour session.

If your group makes the quillow, divide into two groups—cutters and sewers. With just a few volunteers, you'll complete several in 2 hours.

## Supplies for One Patchwork Quillow

- **Coordinating cotton fabrics**—sufficient yardage or pieces to cut out twenty-five 9" x 12" rectangles.

---

*Note from Nancy*

So many of you are looking for something useful to do with extra fabric and tools too precious to throw away. One phone call to a prison, rehabilitation center or just about any community service organization can put those supplies to work helping others.

---

- **1-5/8 yds. of coordinating cotton fabric for the backing.**

- **Cotton embroidery floss or yarn.**

- **1/2 yd. of cotton fabric for pillow.**

- **Batting**—a 45" x 60" piece.

- **Handy notions**—rotary cutter, mat and ruler; 1/4" (0.6 cm) quilting foot (see "Note from Nancy" below right); seam gauge; thread; point turner such as Bamboo Pointer and Creas-er (see page 94 for shopping information); safety pins or size 1 curved basting pins; large-eyed chenille needle; large table space.

### Supplies for One Fleece Quillow

- **1-7/8 yd. of 58"/60" high-loft fleece such as Polarfleece® or Eskimo Fleece.**

- **Handy notions**—rotary cutter, mat and ruler; thread; large table space.

# Patchwork Quillow: Five Simple Steps to Completion

## Step 1: Cut quilt rectangles.

- Press fabrics to remove wrinkles.

- Cut a template from cardboard or a plastic template material. Place the template on the fabric, outline the rectangle shape and use scissors or rotary cutter to cut out the rectangle.

- Or fold the fabric in half and in half again, meeting selvage edges. Align the fabric with the inch markings on the mat. With a rotary cutter, mat and ruler, cut a 12" crosscut. Unfold the fabric and re-cut into 9" rectangles.

- Cut twenty-five 9" x 12" rectangles from coordinating fabrics.
  *(Instructions continue on next page)*

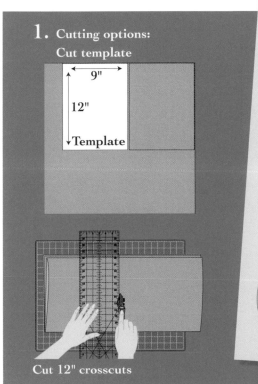

**1. Cutting options:**
Cut template
9"
12"
↓Template

Cut 12" crosscuts

### Note from Nancy

Traditional quilting enthusiasts generally use a 1/4" allowance for seams. Special quilting feet, such as the Little Foot® (see page 94 for shopping information), are exactly 1/4" on each side to gauge the seam perfectly.

A standard presser foot can also be used to achieve a narrow seam allowance —just guide the 1/4" side of the presser foot along the fabric edge.

Little Foot®

Creative Kindness Knows No Walls

www.creativekindness.com

## Step 2: **Stitch the rectangles together.**

- Stitch the rectangles together, seaming the long edges. Use a standard quilting seam allowance of 1/4".
- Sew five rows of five rectangles.
- Press the seam allowances of each row in one direction. To reduce the bulk when joining the rows together, alternate the direction the seams are pressed—press row one to the left, then press row two to the right and so on.
- Stitch the five rows together to make the quillow top. Press the seam allowances in one direction.

## Step 3: **Add the pillow to the backing.**

- Measure the size of the patchwork quillow top (it should measure approximately 43" x 58"). Cut a length of cotton fabric for the backing to fit this measurement.

- From the 1/2 yard of fabric allotted for the pillow, cut an 18" x 36" rectangle. With right sides and the short edges meeting, stitch the side seams and zigzag to finish the unseamed edges. Turn the pillow right side out.

- Fold the backing in half along one short edge to determine the center point; mark with a pin. Fold the unfinished pillow edge in half to determine the center point; mark that spot with a pin.

- Pin the pillow to the right side of the backing, matching center points and raw edges.

- Topstitch the pillow to the backing along the pillow side edges. Restitch the topstitching, especially at the seam ends.

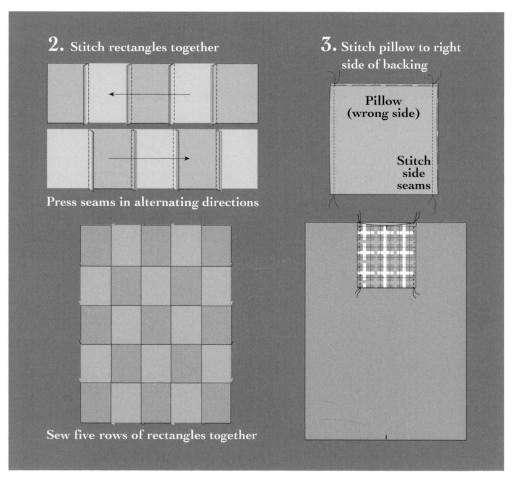

**2.** Stitch rectangles together

Press seams in alternating directions

Sew five rows of rectangles together

**3.** Stitch pillow to right side of backing

Pillow (wrong side)

Stitch side seams

Creative Kindness Knows No Walls

## Step 4: Layer and stitch the quillow.

- Cut a length of quilt batting the same size as the backing.

- Place the batting on a work surface and smooth out. Place the backing on top of the batting with the *right side* of the fabric facing up. Pin the edges together with the pin heads along the outer edges.

- Place the quilt top on top of the backing fabric, *right sides together*. Re-pin all of the layers together along the edges.

- For turning the quilt right side out, mark a 20" opening along one long side. Place two pins next to each other at each end of the opening.

- Stitch the quillow together using a narrow seam allowance. Do not stitch between the double pin area.

- Re-stitch the corners. Trim off the excess seam allowances at the corners, cutting at an angle.

## Step 5: Turn and tie quilt.

- Turn the quilt right side out through the opening.

- Smooth the layers together. Use a point turner to form square corners.

- Pin or safety-pin all the layers together. Do not pin through the pillow.

- Using cotton embroidery floss or yarn in a large-eyed chenille needle, tie the layers together at each seam intersection. Securely knot each tie.

  **Note:** There are two seam intersections in the pillow area. Reach through pillow from back of the quilt to prevent needle from going through pillow layer. *Only tie the layers through the quilt top, batting and backing.*

- Finish the quillow by hand-stitching the opening closed.

- To place the quilt inside the pillow, fold the quilt into thirds lengthwise. Next, fold the quilt into fourths, folding from the end opposite the pillow. Turn the pillow inside out, tucking the folded quilt inside the pillow.

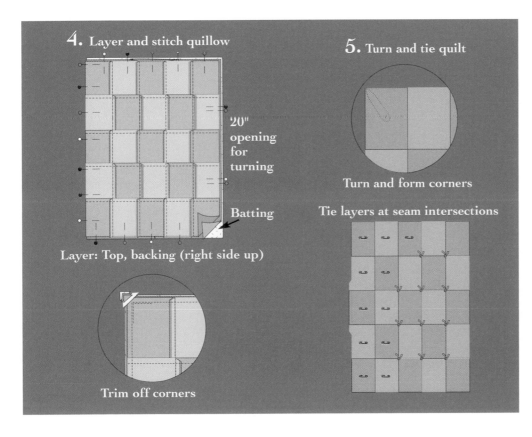

**4.** Layer and stitch quillow

20" opening for turning

Batting

Layer: Top, backing (right side up)

Trim off corners

**5.** Turn and tie quilt

Turn and form corners

Tie layers at seam intersections

*"I am homebound and always enjoy your show. I had a stroke 2 years ago, and before that I enjoyed basic knitting and crocheting. It's been a long way back to be able to write and use the fingers on my right side. Last year at Christmas I had to force my hands to do my therapy by crocheting. I made 74 different items — hats, scarves and slippers — that our church included with food baskets. Your 'Sew a Smile' show has given me ideas for so many projects that help me feel worthwhile and help others."*

Linda
Winchester, Virginia

Creative Kindness Knows No Walls

# Fleece Quillow:
## Two Simple Steps to Completion

### Step 1: Cut quillow sections.

- Trim away the fleece selvages.

- Cut out the blanket and pillow sections as shown in illustration at right. Use the remaining fleece for other projects. (Or use the fabric for the pillows on two additional quillows. You'll only need an extra 1-1/3 yards of fleece for each additional quillow you make.)

### Step 2: Attach the pillow.

- Turn under a 1/2" hem on one of the non-stretchy cut edges of the pillow. Zigzag the hem in place.

- Fold the pillow in half to locate its center. Mark at the cut edge opposite the stitched hem.

- Fold the 48" edge of the blanket in half to locate its center. Mark.

- Place and pin the pillow on the blanket with right sides together, matching the centers.

- Stitch around the three sides of the pillow with a straight stitch or a narrow zigzag as shown at right.

- Place the blanket pillow-side down. Fold the blanket into thirds lengthwise, wrapping the blanket edges toward the wrong side. Next, fold the blanket into fourths, folding from the end opposite the pillow. Turn the pillow right side out, tucking the folded blanket inside.

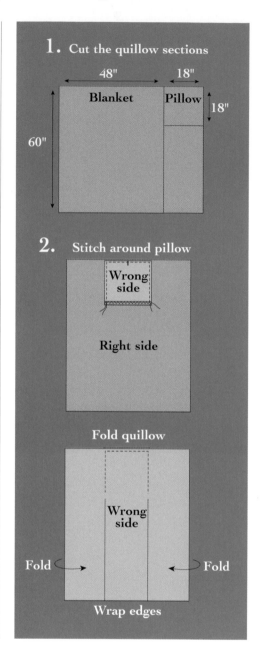

1. Cut the quillow sections

48" — Blanket | 18" — Pillow | 18"

60"

2. Stitch around pillow

Wrong side

Right side

Fold quillow

Wrong side

Fold — Fold

Wrap edges

## How You Can
## Crochet Granny Squares

You can multiply project possibilities—and project portability—with versatile Granny Squares.

One crocheter told us, "That square for a crocheter is like cream of mushroom soup for a cook." In other words, you can do almost anything with it.

The following instructions are for a

solid-color 3" square. (Remember that lighter-weight yarn will yield a smaller square and heavier-weight yarn will yield a larger square.)

## Supplies for a Granny Square

- **Crochet hook, size G or H.**

- **Worsted-weight yarn.** (If using more than one type, try to match care requirements and fiber content.)

## Note from Nancy

Granny squares are a portable crocheted "quilt square" that can be pieced together into a multitude of projects, from clothes for babies to large afghans.

Good news for newcomers to crochet: Because it is worked with one hook and is more stable than knitting, crocheting is less susceptible to the yarn-tension variations that can plague beginners.

Better still, because different colors and textures can be mixed in this patchwork crochet, economical leftover yarn can be used.

*"I was asked by a friend to crochet or knit hats for preemie AIDS babies. I am delighted to help these poor children in this way. I also enjoy sewing. Thanks for all the welcome information you give on your show to help me with my favorite hobby."*

Jacqueline Pikesgrove, New Jersey

# Granny Square: Two Simple "Rounds" to Completion

## Directions

Beginning at center of block, ch 6, sl st in beginning ch to form a ring.

### Round 1

Ch 3, make 2 dcs in ring, catching the loose thread end.

The ch 3 counts as 1 dc on this corner for each round. (Do not make the dcs through the top two threads, which you might be accustomed to doing. Make them through the sp that is formed by the ring.)

* Ch 3, make 3 dcs in ring, repeat from the * two more times. To close the

### Crochet abbreviations

| | |
|---|---|
| ch(s) | chain(s) |
| dc(s) | double crochet(s) |
| hdc(s) | half double crochet(s) |
| lp(s) | loops |
| sl st | slip stitch |
| sp | space |
| st | stitch |

corner, ch 1 and hdc in the top st of the starting ch-3.

*(Instructions continue on next page)*

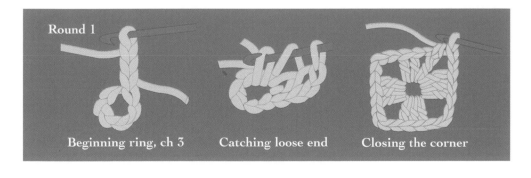

Round 1

Beginning ring, ch 3          Catching loose end          Closing the corner

Creative Kindness Knows No Walls

## Round 2

Ch 3 (for first dc), make 2 dcs in same corner sp, ch 1, make 3 dcs in the next corner sp.

*Ch 3 (for corner), make 3 dcs in the same sp as before, ch 1, make 3 dcs in the next sp, repeat from * two more times. Ch 1 and hdc in the top st of the starting ch-3.

For more rounds, repeat same steps: A group of 3 dcs in each sp with a ch-1 between; in corner spaces, two groups of 3 dcs with a ch-3 between. Begin round; close corner as before.

**To change colors**: (This is done in the hdc with which a round is closed. After you have made the last 3 dcs, ch 1 and you are ready to start.)

Yarn over, draw up a lp in the top st of the starting ch-3 and drop the working yarn. With contrasting color, yarn over and draw through all 3 lps on the hook to complete the hdc. Start your new round, working over loose yarn ends when making the dcs.

**To join the squares**: Squares are generally sewn together with the same yarn and a tapestry needle. Place the wrong sides together and catch the two back lps as shown below center.

Once you master this basic design, try some creative departures:

- Continue making rounds until your square is crib-size or larger.

- Vary color by square for a patch-work look or by round for a rainbow effect. Both methods also use up yarn leftovers effectively.

- For a more pronounced seam, join together squares using a single crochet stitch on the right or wrong side in a matching or contrasting color of yarn.

- Fringe edges easily by holding four to eight strands of yarn together and folding in half to form a lp. Insert the crochet hook from back to front and draw a lp through. Draw the loose ends through the lp and pull tightly to form a knot.

- Combine squares as building blocks for a wide array of fashions and furnishings: sweaters, ponchos, shawls, mufflers, hats, mittens, buntings, blankets and even cuddly toys.

- For other intriguing variations and free patterns, visit our Web site www.creativekindness.com.

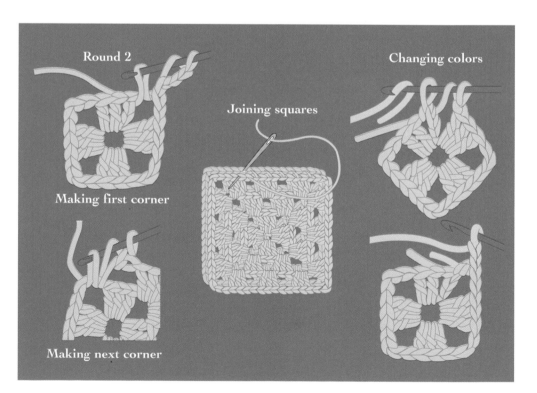

Round 2

Making first corner

Making next corner

Joining squares

Changing colors

Creative Kindness Knows No Walls

# Creative Kindness Continues
## Men Have Helping Hands, Too

IT does not seem unusual that the women of Taycheedah (see page 70) are learning skills traditionally considered feminine. Can you imagine teaching those skills to teenage male offenders, many former gang members?

Anita Hatfield not only imagined it, she has been doing it since 1998 in the Preston Youth Correctional Facility in Ione, California.

### Science and Life Science

Anita is a science teacher in this "school" located about an hour north of Sacramento. Her students, all young men, range in age from 16 to 22.

To watch them intently sewing tiny baby gowns, knitting booties and crocheting blankets, it's hard to believe that these young men are here for criminal offenses.

Anita's students learn to sew, knit and crochet by starting with easy projects. All the items are then donated to Sacramento-area hospitals supported by the Newborns in Need program (see page 11).

Anita's courageous needlework program is not just recreational. One of her goals is to raise the students' self-esteem and sense of accomplishment.

Students also learn about community involvement, the needs of others and the meaning of restitution.

"I'm doing something for a little kid who needs my help," says Jimmy Pinto as he knits an afghan. "This blanket is going to keep someone warm."

Jaimé Felix, another student, is more introspective. As he crochets, he thinks about his son whom he has never seen. "I want to bring happiness, not tears," he says.

This needlework program must also fit into Anita's science curriculum, so nurses and other experts come in to teach about infant health and parenting. And before they can work on their service projects, students must complete their other assignments.

*Anita Hatfield and inmates at the Preston Youth Correctional Facility work on projects for babies.*

Their proud teacher is not at all surprised by the concern, enthusiasm and even love these tough guys show for babies. Anita notes, too, that many students say doing needlework gives them time to think and have fun without getting into trouble.

### Positive Future and Feedback

"We talk about the future," says Jimmy, who plans to finish school and help his family. Jaimé agrees. "Two or three of us talk about teaching crocheting, getting involved and finding out how to help."

Students are getting positive feedback as well. They have been featured in print and television stories, including *People* magazine. One boy boasted to his mom that he made the paper "…for doing something right".

Although it took several years of convincing to get her program off the ground, Anita is grateful for the support and security from the prison administration. She advises anyone interested in starting a similar program to stick with it, work through official channels and abide by security rules.

For anyone considering teaching in a prison setting, Jimmy promises you will find "a lot of people who want to learn. Men and teenagers can do this."

*"Could you let me know what groups were mentioned on the 'Sewing with Nancy' program? I'm anxious to get involved with sewing for good causes and donating some extra fabric and other supplies that I have. Thank you so much."*

Paula
Manassas, Virginia

Creative Kindness Knows No Walls

# Sew for the CURE

Dear Nancy,

I'm part of a sewing guild that has nearly 50 members. We plan "workdays" and have an enjoyable time making lap robes and quilts to donate.

We'd like to add to our list of community service projects. It is a good feeling to help those less fortunate than we are.

Twila
New Sharon, Iowa

"The candlestick in a low place has given light as faithfully as that upon a hill."

Margaret Fuller

# Find Goodness Everywhere

## And in Yourself

WHO would have imagined that there would be so many dedicated and unselfish people quietly helping their neighbors, near and far?

Scores of groups and individuals see children needing comfort, the homeless needing warmth, the sick needing encouragement and the elderly needing companionship—and are moved to take action without expectation of fame or reward.

The silence of their *Creative Kindness* speaks loudly of the human spirit and its capacity for good. Evidence of that goodness is in the stories shared here.

Chances are, if you haven't already, you'll find a cause that touches your heart and projects custom-made for your time and talents.

# Circle of Women

DISTANCE is no obstacle for the Circle of Women, a group among those first featured in my "Sew a Smile" series.

Circle of Women members make quilts for the Lakota Sioux living on the Rosebud Reservation in South Dakota—over 1,200 miles away. Organized by eight women in 1997, these busy seamstresses also provide quilts for needy children in their own community of Troy, Montana.

Founding member Marbie Randall shared an effective resource-building strategy: The group started with only $20 given by a local church, but members wisely used that seed money for a mailing to fabric stores. The stores, in turn, raised about $600 in material donations.

Three years after meeting this group, I received an update. "When we were featured on your 'Sew a Smile' program," wrote Marbie, "we were warned that we would probably only receive donations for about the first 6 months.

"Well, wonder of wonders, we are still receiving donations and have been

*Raven One Star, 13, works on her first quilt in a Lakota Sioux class cooperatively taught by Circle of Women and the Rosebud Reservation quilters.*

gifted with quilt tops, material, finished blocks, thread, quilt books and other basic supplies.

"Plus, because of your program, we have been joined in this labor of love by a lady in Billings, Montana, over 500 miles away. It is because of her that we have also started quilting Christmas stockings.

"Beginning last year, the Troy Methodist Church has been giving us financial support, too. This has enabled us to mail 1,820 pounds of clothing and 32 quilts to the reservation.

"Last year, we started a sister group of Circle of Women on the Rosebud Reservation. These women can quilt! Our group from Troy hopes to visit the reservation in the spring of 2001 and do a week-long workshop with our sister group."

*"Presbyterian Women and four other churches in our area will be sewing for the needy families at the food pantry. They pick up bags of food each week, and now we will also offer some of the 'Sew a Smile' projects. Thank you for your ideas and patterns."*

Billie
(E-mail)

## Note from Nancy

In "Connecting with Charities and Each Other" (page 94), Gail and I explain how to get contact information for all the groups and individuals featured in this section and throughout this book.

# Rosie's Calico Cupboard Quilt Shop

ROSIE GONZALEZ, owner of Rosie's Calico Cupboard Quilt Shop in San Diego, California, can best be described as a woman of action.

One day, she was talking to someone

from the local American Cancer Society office about "Camp Reach for the Sky" for kids battling cancer. Rosie said to herself, "These kids deserve a quilt...", and she was off and running.

Find Goodness Everywhere

This tireless shop owner relies on a network of volunteers to make the 200 quilts a year needed to give every camper a quilt. She asks schoolchildren to make blocks as a class project and local quilting groups and guilds to contribute quilt tops.

Her vendors are asked to donate fabric and batting. Customers and staff members attend sew-a-thons, where they add borders and bind the quilts.

For the actual quilting, Rosie and the owner of a nearby quilting machine shop had a bright idea—let customers who purchase a quilt machine practice on the "Reach for the Sky" quilts.

Each child gets to keep his or her own twin-size blanket, which is sent with "a prayer in every stitch" and a message of love and hope. Quilts are given to campers at the July (ages 4 to 8) and August (ages 8 to 19) sessions.

Rosie reports that even though the

*Young cancer patients at "Camp Reach for the Sky" eagerly look through a pile of bright handmade quilts to pick out their own special blanket.*

group does not start sewing until November for the next year's camps, many volunteers want to keep quilting all year long.

# *Loving Hands Quilts*

AUTO ACCIDENTS are traumatic enough for adults—imagine the terror that children feel. Helen Preiss and the Loving Hands Quilts group are part of a cooperative effort with the Missouri Highway Patrol to help kids find comfort and security after roadway collisions.

Every time a child under 10 is involved in an accident, the patrol officer

*(Left to right) Helen Preiss, Lois Ebel and Marilyn Webert help lead Loving Hands Quilts.*

is able to give him or her a quilt to hang on to throughout the trauma. The quilt is the child's to keep.

One highway patrolman reported that he once had to deliver a baby and wrap it in the only "cover" he had—a Missouri road map. He now carries handmade quilts at all times, as do other Missouri law enforcement personnel and ambulance attendants.

Loving Hands members estimate that their annual need is nearly 1,500 quilts, keeping 200 to 300 in reserve. Anyone can help them reach their goal, Helen notes. Non-sewers can lend a hand, too, by picking up and delivering the supplies and quilts.

There are now nine Loving Hands troops in Missouri. Helen and two other leaders from Troop C, Marilyn Webert and Lois Ebel, divided the state into regions by county and established drop-off points for donations.

As these busy women say, "The need for quilts is never-ending."

*"I watch your show whenever I can and appreciate your sharing 'Sew a Smile'. My 9-year-old son has been battling cancer for 4-1/2 years now, and I have spent a great deal of time at the hospital. I take my sewing machine with me and set up shop. Many of the nurses are also sewers, and we share ideas. How nice it would be if we could work toward some common goal for helping others."*

Pam
Everett, Washington

Find Goodness Everywhere

SOMETIMES a life-threatening experience opens a door to creative opportunity. It did for Verda Campbell of Naples, Florida.

"After I had breast surgery in 1985, there was only one nurse who could make me comfortable. I could hardly

*Verda Campbell (right) delivers a "Bosom Pals Pillow" to Christina Battisti of Sterling, Virginia, who plans to give it to her sister-in-law in Texas.*

wait for her to come in — she knew just where to put the pillow.

"After taking a few ugly overstuffed pillows along when I visited other patients, I designed a soft, just-right pillow for others."

Verda's heart-shaped design is made of soft fabric and features a special underarm fit. Finished with the signature pink ribbon loop, these pillows offer more than physical comfort to breast cancer patients — they represent hope and a reminder that they are not alone.

Verda has made hundreds of pillows herself and organized her church group to make more. Through the American Cancer Society's "Reach for Recovery" program, there are now groups in Texas and Arkansas that also make "Bosom Pals Pillows".

"The volunteers have been so moved that we are now sending a little prayer along with each pillow," says Verda. "They realize cancer affects all of us."

*"I have three barrels of fabric and two barrels of yarn from my mom's estate. I've been trying to decide what is best to do with this. Now I know! 'Sew a Smile'! When I get settled, I'll ask some of the local ladies to join me and decide just which projects would benefit our community. Thank you so much for spreading the word. We need so much more kindness and giving in all our lives."*

Phyllis
Kennewick,
Washington

## How You Can Quickly Assemble
# A Bosom Pals Pillow

**If you make the pillow(s):** Plan on allotting 30 minutes for each five-step pillow project.

**If your group makes the pillow(s):** Each group member or team can specialize in a certain step or steps. If some group members don't sew, they can still cut out, turn, press or stuff the pillows.

### Supplies for One Pillow

- **Bosom Pals Pillow pattern** (on page 85).

- **1/2 yd. (0.5 m) white cotton or cotton-blend fabric, 45" (115 cm) wide.** Variations: Choose a print (muted or bright) or, for a really different look, high-loft fleece. Match the trim to the fabric color,

texture and weight.

- **Matching all-purpose thread.**

- **Polyester fiberfill.**

- **Optional** — 2/3 yd. (0.6 m) of pink ribbon, 1/4" (0.6 cm) wide; 1/2 yd. (0.5 m) of white beading with a floral design, 3/4" (2 cm) wide.

# Bosom Pals Pillow:
## Five Simple Steps to Completion

### Step 1: Cut out the heart.

- Use a photocopier to enlarge the heart pattern below.

- Cut out heart pattern. Cut out two fabric hearts for each pillow.

*(Instructions continue on next page)*

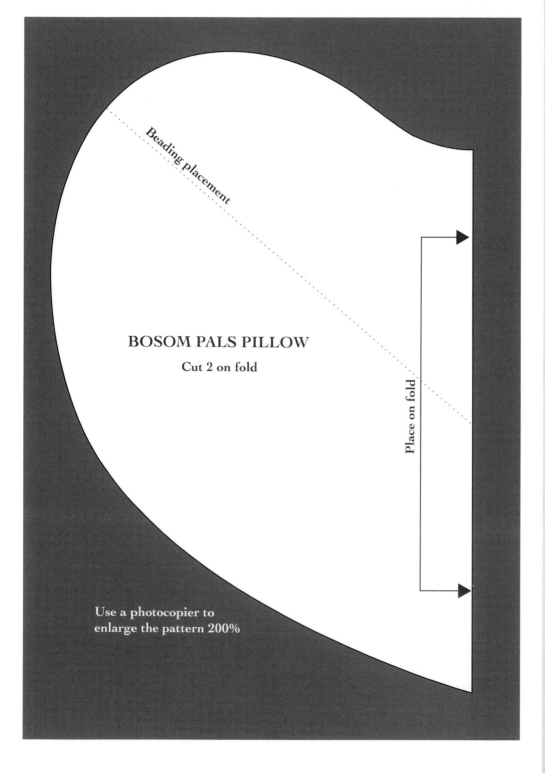

Beading placement

**BOSOM PALS PILLOW**

Cut 2 on fold

Place on fold

Use a photocopier to enlarge the pattern 200%

*"We make stuffed bears for police and firemen to give to kids in crisis situations. So far, our local Girl Scouts have had three workshops and have made a ton of bears."*

Lori
(E-mail)

Find Goodness Everywhere

## Step 2: Add ribbon beading (optional).

- Weave pink ribbon through beading. Cut off excess ribbon.

- Position the beading and ribbon on the right side of one of the pillow sections as indicated on the pattern. Edgestitch both sides of the beading in place.

- Shape the remaining ribbon to look like the breast cancer symbol. Machine-tack in place.

## Step 3: Join the front and back of the pillow.

- Place the pillow front on top of the pillow back, right sides together, and sew using a 1/4" seam allowance. Leave a 3"-4" (12.5 cm-15 cm) opening on one side for turning and stuffing the pillow.

## Step 4: Turn the pillow right side out.

- Trim and grade the seam as needed.

- Turn through opening.

## Step 5: Stuff the pillow.

- Insert fiberfill, adding enough to create a soft surface.

- Hand-stitch opening closed.

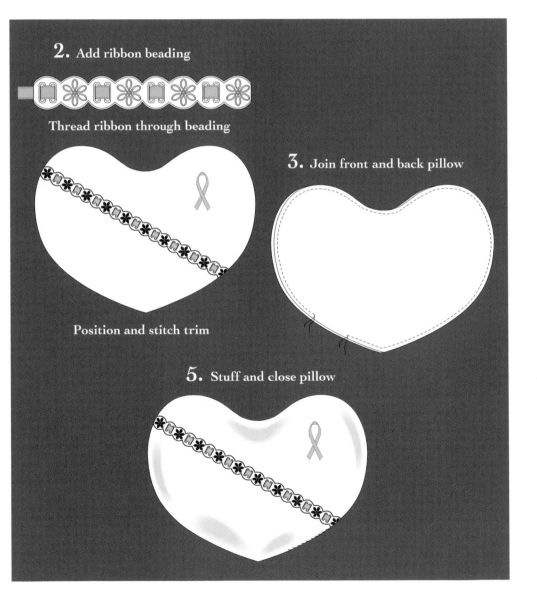

**2.** Add ribbon beading

Thread ribbon through beading

Position and stitch trim

**3.** Join front and back pillow

**5.** Stuff and close pillow

Find Goodness Everywhere

# Alexa's Hat Company

WHAT do a class of very hip middle-schoolers and a cancer treatment center have in common? Teacher Margaret Januzzi's Home Economics/Life Development students at Anderson Junior High School in Chandler, Arizona know the answer.

In 1993, the 6-year-old niece of Margaret's best friend was diagnosed with cancer. "Alexa lost her hair to chemotherapy, and small hats were hard to find," Margaret recalls. "I felt my sewing class could help."

"Alexa's Hat Company" was started and run by the class as a real manufacturing business. Their product? "Kids' Kindness Kaps"—baseball hats for juvenile cancer victims like Alexa.

Not only did the students learn sewing skills, but also cancer awareness and caring for others. Another important goal of the program was to build self-esteem, both for the teens sewing the hats and the kids receiving them.

To streamline production, Margaret limited students to one or two styles. No matter what pattern you choose, she notes, the design should cover the head well and feel soft next to delicate skin. Beyond that, however, the wilder and brighter the caps, the more they appeal to their "customers".

As part of the lesson plan, students also went on a tour of the local cancer

*Each group member can create one complete cap or specialize in one step of the assembly process.*

treatment center, where they learned about different types of cancer and saw medical equipment designed especially for children.

Upon seeing a teenager attached to IV tubes, one of Margaret's students remarked, "He is our age. He could be a friend of mine." For this teen, cancer had taken on a familiar face.

Another student summed up the experience beautifully. "I learned a lot through Alexa's Hat Company. I learned about giving to people and not expecting anything back.

"We had fun making hats and going down to the cancer center to give them away. Most of all, I learned that people really do care. I do, the nurses and doctors do and all the volunteers do.

"With love, faith and care, people can help these children survive."

*"Kids' Kindness Kaps" truly have kid appeal — they're trendy, bright and instantly easy to wear.*

*Note from Nancy*

Building on the Alexa's Hat Company experience, Margaret has established the "Eclipse Embroidery Design Company" so her students can market their skills to area businesses.

Oh yes, an update on Alexa: She's recovered and doing well.

*"I am undergoing chemotherapy for lymphoma cancer. I hopefully have just one more treatment to go. The Lord has greatly blessed me—I haven't had any sickness or hair loss. The only effect I have is tiredness! I belong to our local quilt guild and the American Sewing Guild. I am very interested in helping others get through their sickness. Bless you for all that you do."*

Rose
Arnold,
Pennsylvania

Here's a great project for kids to sew for other kids in need of head coverings. Remember to use fun, bright novelty prints!

**If you make the cap(s):** Each of the five steps will take approximately 10-15 minutes, for a total of 50-75 minutes for each cap.

**If your group makes the cap(s):** Each group member or team can specialize in a certain step or steps. If some group members don't sew, they can cut out the pieces and press.

## Supplies for One Kids' Kindness Kap

- **3/8 yd. each (0.35 m) cotton fashion fabric and cotton lining,** 44/45" (115 cm) wide.

- **1/4 yd. (0.25 m) heavyweight fusible interfacing** (such as Shir-Tailor® by Pellon).

- **Matching all-purpose thread.**

- **Kids' Kindness Kap pattern** (on page 89). Change the size by decreasing (to enlarge) or increasing (to downsize) the seam width.

> *"Even in my small community, I see too many relatively young women suffering from hair loss. They are too youthful and attractive to wear dowdy hats or wigs. Your baseball caps would be perfect for them, and I know their children would love them. I can't wait to get started."*
>
> Ivy
> (E-mail)

## Kids' Kindness Kap: Five Simple Steps to Completion

### Step 1: Cut out the pattern pieces.

- Use photocopier to enlarge patterns on page 89. Cut out patterns.

### Step 2: Lay out the pattern; cut out the fabric sections.

- Cut out two or more caps at the same time.

- From the cotton fashion fabric, cut six crown pieces and two brim pieces (for each cap).

- From the lining fabric, cut six crown pieces (for each cap).

- From heavyweight interfacing, cut two brim pieces (for each cap).

- Mark the center of the brim with a fabric marking pen or pencil. *(Instructions continue on page 90)*

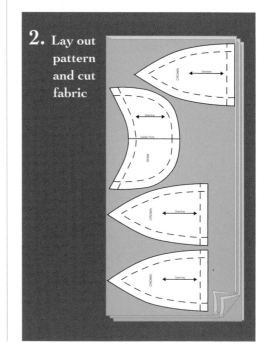

2. Lay out pattern and cut fabric

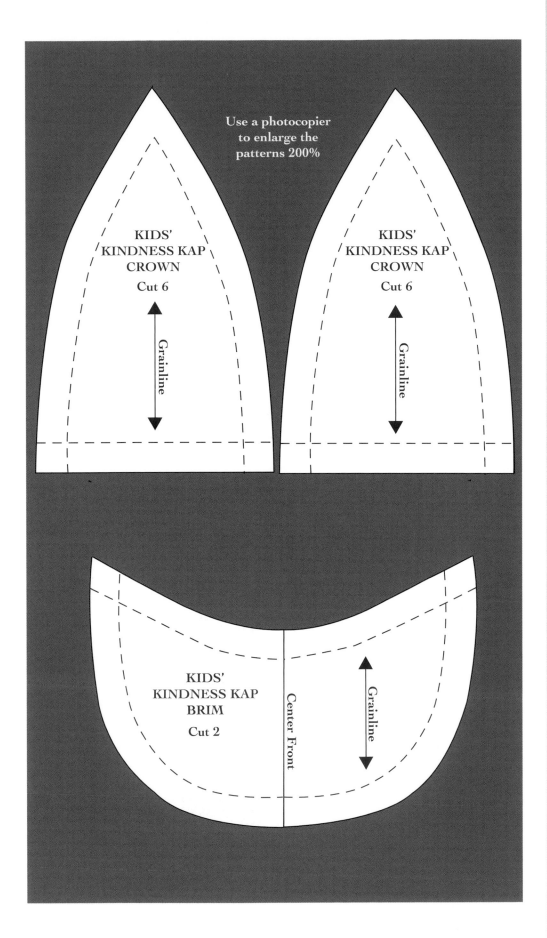

Use a photocopier
to enlarge the
patterns 200%

KIDS'
KINDNESS KAP
CROWN

Cut 6

Grainline

KIDS'
KINDNESS KAP
CROWN

Cut 6

Grainline

KIDS'
KINDNESS KAP
BRIM

Cut 2

Center Front

Grainline

Find Goodness Everywhere

www.creativekindness.com

## Step 3: Stitch the cap crown.

- Stitch the long sides of two crown sections, right sides together. Trim the seam allowances to 1/4" (0.6 cm) and press to one side. Add a third crown piece in the same way.

- Repeat, stitching a second three-piece crown section.

- Stitch the two crown halves, right sides together.

- Assemble the lining in the same way, leaving an opening for turning.

- Fold the crown in half, matching seams. Mark one fold for the cen-ter front and the other for the center back.

- Mark the center of the brim with a fabric marking pen or pencil.

## Step 4: Stitch the brim.

- Fuse interfacing to the wrong side of each brim piece.

- Pin and stitch brim pieces, right sides together, as shown below.

- Grade the seam allowances by cutting to graduated widths, close to stitching. Notch the curve to reduce bulk.

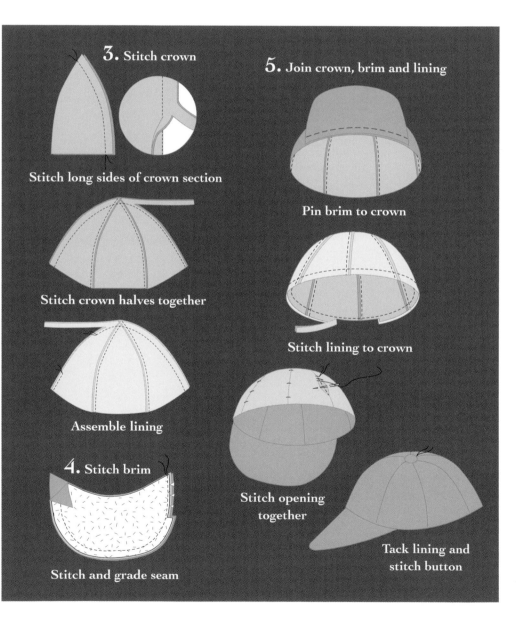

**3. Stitch crown**

Stitch long sides of crown section

Stitch crown halves together

Assemble lining

**4. Stitch brim**

Stitch and grade seam

**5. Join crown, brim and lining**

Pin brim to crown

Stitch lining to crown

Stitch opening together

Tack lining and stitch button

Find Goodness Everywhere

- Turn the brim right side out and smooth out the stitched curves. Press the brim. Machine-baste the cut edges together.

## Step 5: Join the crown, brim and crown lining.

- Pin the brim to the crown with right sides together, making sure to match center fronts. Baste the brim to the crown.

- With right sides together, pin the lining to the crown (over brim), matching seams. Stitch. Trim the seam allowance to 1/4" (0.6 cm).

- Turn the cap right side out through the opening. Press the seam. Slip-stitch the opening edges together.

- Tack the lining to the crown seam to prevent shifting.

- Stitch a button to the top of the hat where all seams meet.

# *Creative Kindness Continues*
## More Project Possibilities

WE could have written about literally hundreds of stories in this chapter—each one heartwarming, each project creative, each need important.

You can find more stories and projects on our Web site (www.creative kindness.com) and, we hope, discover how to develop your own brand of *Creative Kindness*.

Here, we've included our *Creative Kindness* Pillow, featured on the front cover of this book. With a special note tucked in the pocket, the pillow serves as a soft greeting card to those in need.

# How You Can Quickly Assemble
## *Our Creative Kindness Pillow*

**If you make the pillow(s)**: Each step will take 10-15 minutes, so one pillow can be made in under an hour.

**If your group makes the pillow(s)**: Each group member or team can specialize in a certain step or steps. If some group members don't sew, they can cut out, turn, press and stuff the pillows.

### Supplies for One Pillow

- *Creative Kindness* Pillow pattern (on page 93).

- 1/3 yd. (0.30 m) fabric, 44/45" (112/115 cm) wide (for base).

- 1/8 yd. (0.15 m) contrasting-color fleece fabric (for heart).

- Polyester fiberfill.

- Matching all-purpose thread.

- 1/4" (0.6 cm) wide ribbon (optional).

*(Instructions continue on next page)*

# *Creative Kindness* Pillow:
## Three Simple Steps to Completion

### Step 1: Trace and cut out *two* heart pieces.

- Trace the pattern on page 93. Trace two patterns for faster cutting.

- Fold the fleece in half, meeting selvages. Position the patterns on the fleece; cut out the heart pieces.

- Fold the base fabric, meeting selvages; cut out four 9-1/2" (24.3 cm) square pillow bases.

### Step 2: Applique the pocket.

- Open one pair of half hearts, right sides up. Meet points, aligning overlapping sides.

- Position and pin the heart diagonally on one pillow base.

- Stitch around the heart, catching both layers where the pocket over-

laps. Use a straight, zigzag, blanket or decorative stitch. If you use a decorative stitch, be sure to add a stabilizer to prevent the fleece from stretching.

### Step 3: Sew and finish the pillow.

- Place the pillow front on top of back, right sides together. Straight-stitch a 1/4" (0.6 cm) seam along one edge of the pillow, sewing from edge to edge.

- Fold the seam along the stitching

*"I am a grade 7 and 8 home economics teacher in a Catholic high school. The students here have a community service component in their religious values course. I am hoping to complete some of your projects in class."*

Anne-Marie
(E-mail)

## Note from Nancy

The technique of "wrapping" the corners may be new to you. It's an easy way to eliminate grading and produces a less puckered, more durable and less pointed corner.

**1.** Cut out heart pieces from fleece

HALF HEART
for Support Pillow pocket
Cut 2

overlap line

heart point

HALF HEART
for Support Pillow pocket
Cut 2

overlap line

heart point

**2.** Pin and stitch heart

**3.** Stitch and "wrap" corners

line. The seam allowance will "wrap" toward the inside of the pillow.

- Beginning at the fold, stitch a 1/4" (0.6 cm) seam along the next edge. This makes a "wrapped corner".

- Repeat, wrapping and stitching each of the corners in sequence, leaving a 3"-4" (12.5 cm-15 cm) opening on the final side for turning and stuffing pillow.

- Insert fiberfill.

- Hand-stitch opening closed.

- Slip a card or note into the pocket.

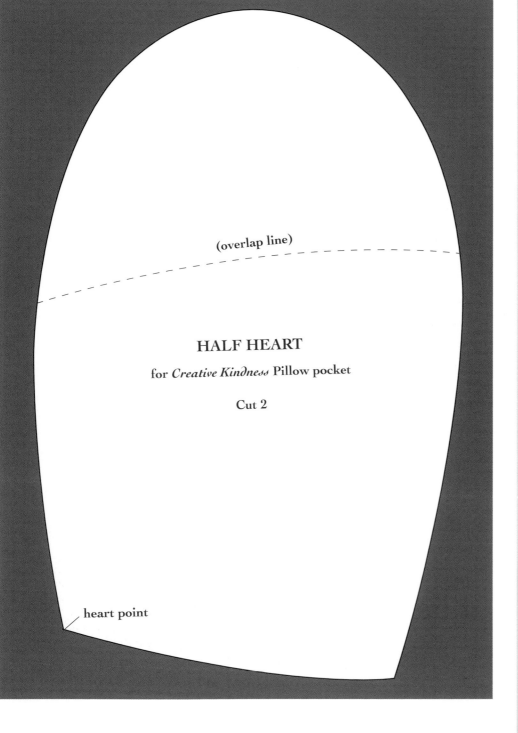

(overlap line)

**HALF HEART**

for *Creative Kindness* Pillow pocket

**Cut 2**

heart point

Find Goodness Everywhere

www.creativekindness.com

# Bring Creative Kindness into Your Life

THE GENEROUS PEOPLE and groups featured in this book share an abundance of motivation, talent and love—all of which are critical to helping them share *Creative Kindness* with so many and in so many ways.

For most of these volunteers, the nature of their work also requires a wide variety and a steady stream of resources. Yet their own resources are often limited.

Those who offer *Creative Kindness* depend on the kindness of others to keep all the needed supplies, funds and projects coming in. You can help, and here's how.

## Via Mail:
## Send Postal Mail or E-Mail

With few exceptions, Gail and I have not included contact numbers for the charities featured in this book. Why? Because they are volunteers or volunteer-based groups with frequently changing addresses, phone, fax and E-mail numbers.

In an effort to be current, we are offering our *Creative Kindness* Reference List both on our Web site (www.creativekindness.com) and by mail (see "Where to Find Our *Creative Kindness* Reference List" on page 95).

Initially, the best way to contact a group is by mail—either postal or E-mail. Allow time for responses—you are usually mailing to individuals, not staffed offices.

If you do call, please be considerate. All of these very busy volunteers are trying to stretch their hours and dollars. Watch for time zone differences and do not call collect or expect people to play long-distance phone tag.

- **When requesting project instructions or patterns**:

Whether you make your request by mail, phone, fax or Internet, always send the individual or group an envelope addressed to yourself and stamped with the correct postage.

Some people and charities may also request a small donation to cover costs.

(Although the patterns may be free, the sender must still pay for envelopes, copying and postage.)

- **When donating cash or materials:**

Contact the potential recipients to verify the address, shipping details and the type of donation. If they cannot use your material donations, don't be offended; most have specific needs and are short on storage space.

Please pack items securely and cover all shipping costs. Of course, donations of checks are always welcomed. (Some, but not all, recipients provide tax-deduction receipts for both material and cash donations.)

---

*"When we were featured on your 'Sew a Smile' program, we were warned that we would probably only receive donations for about the first 6 months. Well, wonder of wonders, we are still receiving donations and have been gifted with quilt tops, material, finished blocks, thread, quilt books and other basic supplies. Beginning last year, the Troy Methodist Church has been giving us financial support, too. This has enabled us to mail 1,820 pounds of clothing and 32 quilts."*

Marbie
Troy, Montana

# Via the Internet:
# Visit Our *Creative Kindness* Web Site

## *Note from Nancy*

There's no problem if you don't have a connection to the Internet at home. You can still visit our Creative Kindness Web site. With few exceptions, public libraries offer Internet access and staff to assist you.

Generally, you can print out pages of interest, although there may be a nominal charge. Schools, senior centers, church groups and even some businesses often permit Internet use, too.

● Get the most up-to-date information on groups, projects, needs, supply sources and donation destinations from the *Creative Kindness* Reference List— and more—on our Web site: www.creativekindness.com.

● This site will showcase a number of charities not featured in the book as well as those that are. Visit often—the site will be updated frequently.

● Read more *Creative Kindness* stories that will touch your heart, inspire your imagination and energize you into action.

● Check out project ideas, hints for maximizing resources, help on getting yourself or a group started and other useful tips.

● See the smiles that make *Creative Kindness* truly rewarding—and contagious.

*"I wanted you to know how much I appreciated the program on community service projects. I suspect the recipients of the work aren't the only people benefiting from the gifts. The givers are equally blessed. I am going to network your project ideas to some friends I think will be interested. Your Web site is very nice, too. I will be going to the Web site for several related projects I'm working on. Thank you."*

Rae
Kansas City, Missouri

# Where to Find Our
# *Creative Kindness* Reference List

The *Creative Kindness* Reference List is available on our Web site (www.creativekindness.com). You can also receive a free copy of the list by mail— just send us a self-addressed stamped envelope (first class postage, please).

Mail to: Creative Kindness, c/o Nancy's Notions, P.O. Box 683, Beaver Dam WI 53916. We'll add new information to the Reference List periodically as your involvement and the spirit of *Creative Kindness* grows.

Connecting with Charities and Each Other

# *In closing…*

Gail told me a story about a group of people faced with a dilemma. They were all seated at a dining table full of luscious food, but they couldn't eat because their outstretched arms were bound to splints.

Rather than trying, futilely, to feed themselves, they resorted to creativity and kindness—they turned, food in hand, to feed each other.

Sometimes, when typing in the quiet of a late night, I marveled at how closely that story relates to the people, projects and power of *Creative Kindness*. When we reach out to nurture our neighbor, we also feed our souls…we will not hunger.

Thank you for caring and sharing,

*Nancy Zieman and Gail Brown*